Praise for Restart

"Restart challenges leaders to question everything about their business model. Those that do, and are willing to act, will flourish through good times and bad."

- Aaron Jagdfeld, CEO, Generac

"Restart is the must-have book for small businesses seeking to grow during challenging times."

- Kevin Kaufman, Small Business Development Center at UW-Whitewater

"Going back to business as usual and just cutting overheard is easy but just plain dangerous for small businesses right now. It is time to look at all facets of your business, develop new ideas and test, test, test. That is the only way you will grow. Restart shows you how."

- Frank Siebrecht, Mentor, SCORE - SE Wisconsin

"Our company has survived downturns through the great depression, 2000, 2008 and now the current pandemic. Each time we faced a major economic shift that impacted our business we took a new look at new markets that no one else was considering. Restart forces you to do the same thing and gives you the methods to do it."

- Craig Jorgensen, CEO, VJS Construction Services

"My ad agency is in the business of generating new ideas for our clients... who are frequently in high-pressure situations. Most small businesses are in this pressure cooker now too. Restart is a practical read with hard-hitting ideas you can implement right away."

- Clay Cooper, Partner Plan B

"I have always sought out businesses to acquire that have opportunities to innovate and have a huge upside but have not yet uncorked that opportunity. Gee, interviewed companies that have innovated and thrived. This is an important business book for small business owners, especially now."

- Jim Lindenberg, CEO,
Lindy Enterprises

"I love working with startups and small businesses and helping them discover new ways to grow. Restart is a dynamic tool that offers new ideas that can be implemented in your business today."

- Kathy Hust, Angel Investor,
Board Member and Business Advisor

"I am so glad Dave wrote Restart. Small businesses in any industry can use these insights to grow. My business is always seeking new ways to innovate and grow...frankly we are going to be using some of his ideas too!"

- Jerry David, CEO, and Founder
Prescient Financial Solutions

"When Dave came to me about the idea behind Restart...that the best companies are willing to put themselves under the microscope and have the courage to pivot I just smiled. He created a must-read."

- Aaron Hirschmann, President, and Owner
Plas-Tech Engineering

"I thought the idea for Restart was very timely. It points out the importance for business owners to think more entrepreneurially. To stay competitive, businesses need to continually look for new paradigms that may open up new markets, expand delivery systems, create better supply chains, and surround themselves with the very best talent."

- Jim Caldwell, CEO, First Citizens Bank

"I see so many small businesses that are not adapting fast enough. You need to ask your customers what information they want and how they want it...YouTube, Zoom, whatever they want. Gee dives right in and shows small businesses how to do it."

- Tyson Ray, Founding Partner, FORM Wealth Advisors

Thank you to Dad, Mom, Amy, Lindsey and Steven for Your Support…

Restart

The Small Business Guide to Thriving During Chaos

Dave Gee

© 2020 Startup Guides LLC | Publisher: Startup Guides LLC

Website: startupguides.io | Inquiries: info@startupguides.io

Copyright © 2020 All rights reserved. No portion of this book may be reproduced mechanically, electronically, or by any other means without written permission of Startup Guides, LLC. Requests to the publisher for permission should be sent on the "Contact Us" form at: startupguides.io

Content and copy editing by Alexandra Aulisi
Cover design and graphic design by Holtan Ventures
Copy editing by Michael Spanjar

Startup Guides, LLC books are available at special discounts when purchased in bulk for premiums and sales promotions as well as for fundraising or educational use. Special editions or book excerpts can also be created to specification. For details, use the "Contact Us" form at startupguides.io

Disclaimer: The publisher, author, interviewees, and contributing authors have used their best efforts in creating this book. They make no representations or warranties with respect to the accuracy or completeness of the contents of this book and specifically disclaim any implied warranties of merchantability or fitness for a particular purpose. The advice and strategies contained herein may not be suitable for your situation. Neither the publisher, nor the author, nor contributing authors, nor interviewees, shall be liable for any loss of profit or any other commercial damages, including but not limited to special, incidental, consequential, or other damages. The book is sold with the understanding that the publisher, author, interviewees and contributing authors are not engaged in rendering legal, accounting, marketing, or other professional services.

Printed in the United States of America | First printing in June 2020

Book available on Amazon in a digital edition and paperback.

ISBN: 9798643738176

June 18, 2020 – Sixth Edition

A Personal Message to Small Businesses

I'm writing this to you from the perspective of someone that has started and managed three businesses, spent 20 years working for Fortune 500 companies, taught in the MBA program at the University of Wisconsin-Madison, coached hundreds of startups and small businesses, authored two books and managed the Launch Pad startup accelerator at the University of Wisconsin-Whitewater.

As a small business leader, you might have always "been in control" of your life and business, or so you thought. The business you started, purchased, joined or inherited had definite bumps in the road. Sometimes you worried about how you would make payroll. You kept your "game face" on when you came into the office so that your employees had their peace of mind. Yet you hadn't slept the night before. A big customer was paying late, you discovered that finding committed and talented employees was a constant battle, you lost a large account, you just had a blow-up with your business partner, you tapped your entire line of credit, a key supplier went out of business, you were thinking about which employees you would let go first during a cash crunch ... or, just maybe, you wondered if all the stress was worth it anymore. I've been there too.

You might have even successfully navigated the economic challenges of 2000 or 2008 (or both!) but now you have to deal with the fallout from the Coronavirus pandemic. How could you have planned for it? This crisis goes way beyond an economic disaster - it has killed innocent people the world over, disrupted countries, states, cities, communities, and most likely has had some negative impact on your small business.

I wrote this book, *Restart*, to help small businesses thrive during and after chaos. I've conducted interviews with highly successful business leaders that will provide insights that you won't get anywhere else. These interviews encompass a variety of sectors, including: angel investing, banking, construction, consulting, economic development, financial services, insurance, restaurants, retail, hospitality, manufacturing, sports, technology, telecommunications, wealth management, and more. The combination of these insights along with the implementation of proven best practices in small business innovation can help your business thrive in the midst of chaos.

So, let's get started!

-Dave

Table of Contents

Three Strategic Paths During Times of Chaos	11
Most Effective Use of this Guide	14
Step 1 – Developing New Business Model Options	16
Step 2 – Marketing Your Small Business	55
Step 3 – Legally Protecting Your Small Business	90
Step 4 – Raising Capital for Your Small Business	110
Step 5 – Selecting Powerful Small Business Software	121
Step 6 – Growing Small Business Ecommerce Sales	124
Step 7 – Building the Ultimate Small Business Team	141
Step 8 – Creating Small Business Pilots	156
Step 9 – Managing Small Business Cash Flow	167
Step 10 – Pivoting to Thrive	180
In Conclusion	186
Glossary	187
About the Author	198

Three Strategic Paths During Times of Chaos

Small businesses around the world have been thrown into a tailspin trying to manage their businesses through the Coronavirus pandemic. This is not the first time that small businesses have experienced economic upheaval and unfortunately, it won't be the last. You have three paths to choose from: you could walk away – shut down your company and be done with it; you could take the standard approach and cut costs to try to stay afloat; or, you can take a new approach and thrive.

Path 1) Dive:

Some small businesses will make the strategic choice to close, merge, or sell their business. They want to **dive** out. And this is a completely valid choice for some. These small businesses owners might no longer have the energy to fight the day-to-day battles, they have run out of cash and don't want to invest more in their business, it's possible that their business models aren't viable anymore, or they simply want to cash out. **This is the safest choice for small businesses to make and comes with the lowest risk.** It could, also, provide them immediate personal cash and likely minimize their stress.

Path 2) Survive:

Many small businesses will attempt to return to business as usual, hoping to restore the status quo and implement some new safeguards against future chaos. The goal of these small businesses is to survive. They might reduce their workforce or just implement furloughs, cut back on product offerings, reduce their previous emphasis on customer service, use lower-cost ingredients, get their suppliers to make price concessions, close offices, or retail locations. The challenge with this path is that, even though they may keep their head above water, their businesses have not adapted their changing environment so, eventually, their business models will become unsustainable. This is the path that is *perceived* to be the least risky and lowest stress but, in actuality, is the most dangerous of the three strategies because it ignores the need for adaptability. People who follow this path often have a Fixed Mindset. *

* A Fixed Mindset, people believe their qualities are **fixed** traits and therefore cannot change.

Path 3) Thrive:

Resilient and adaptable small businesses will make the strategic choice to **thrive**. The decision to thrive takes focus, energy, and investments in their business. These small business owners will think like successful entrepreneurs. They will reassess their business model, will openly assess the challenges the business is facing, analyze the new market in which they operate, talk to existing and new prospective customers for insights and new opportunities, will become laser-focused on new, potential opportunities, review their current products and services, implement efficient and effective marketing methods, innovate, incorporate new technologies, analyze their teams' capabilities, rapidly test new products, services, and processes, and pivot their business models as necessary in order to **thrive.**

Frankly, this path is riskier in the short-term because it requires an investment in time and possibly even money. It will probably create some short-term stress as well. But companies that follow this path will "future proof"* their business for the next crisis. They will also create a sustainable competitive advantage over businesses that simply chose to Survive (path 2, above). Small businesses who choose the Thrive path have a Growth Mindset** and are taking immediate control in order to **"Restart."**

* Future-proofing is the process of anticipating the future and developing methods of minimizing the effects of shocks and stresses of future events. - Wikipedia

** A Growth Mindset is a Mindset that is based on the belief that your basic qualities are things you can cultivate through your efforts.

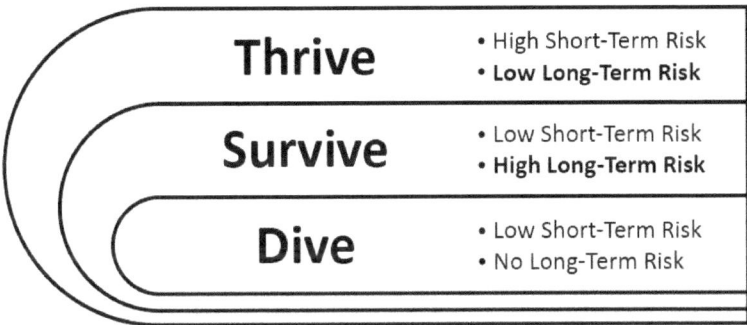

Restart is a step-by-step book for those small businesses that are choosing the **Thrive Strategic Path.** *Restart* provides a **practical step-by-step guide** that you can implement immediately in your small business. This path requires you to step back and take an honest, comprehensive look at your small business and be willing to create a new plan. In some cases, an entirely new vision and or creative strategies may be necessary so you can move forward and thrive in this new environment.

Let's begin!

Most Effective Use of this Guide

The topics covered in this book are presented in chronological order from analyzing your current business model through pivoting your business model for the future. This sequence is proven to provide the best results as each step builds on the previous.

Restart is a workbook – not a textbook filled with theory. You are holding a step-by-step guide that, if utilized correctly, will help your small business thrive during chaos, both now and in the future. Read a section, apply the information, then come back to the book to move on to the next section.

Even if you feel you and your company have already mastered knowledge in a specific area (for example, if you already have a strong marketing presence online), at least skim the section. Despite your previous successes, it is possible that your strategies and tactics need to modernize or adapt to the current environment and future crises.

Restart contains knowledge used by businesses that have successfully navigated chaos and come out stronger for the effort. These are companies, like yours, that had extremely limited time and, sometimes, limited money to develop new business models, test those models, pivot, and thrive – but they did it, and so can you. By using this book, you will build the skills needed to navigate the market dynamics created by the Coronavirus pandemic and it will help you and your team development skills to navigate future crises.

You will probably find information in this book that will be critical to share with your team. In addition to sharing the book with them, we also offer free insights and training which are available at: restartsmallbiz.com. These resources are all practical, engaging, and affordable and will help you acquire knowledge and build the skills necessary to drive growth for your small business.

Before you begin reading, we recommend that you review the Glossary section in the back of the book to familiarize yourself with critical terminology for the modern and thriving small business.

Step 1 – Developing New Business Model Options

The first step toward Thriving in chaos is learning to be adaptable. And, accepting an adaptation to your business model* can be difficult. Most small business owners are very "married" to how their business works and the idea of changing that model can be stressful. However, an honest assessment of your current business model and how well it serves you during chaos is imperative.

Throughout this book, we'll be using the following definition of a business model:

***Business Model**– All of the methods used by a company to deliver value to its customers.

Assuming that your business has been affected by the current pandemic crisis, some of these thoughts may be on your mind:

1. Who should I let go to save money?
2. Should I just cut back the hours of some employees?
3. Maybe I should reduce the hours at the shop?
4. Can I get my supplies any cheaper?
5. Should I close the store?
6. Do I need to extend my line of credit at the bank?
7. Maybe we should start discounting our services?
8. Can I outsource some of our work?
9. Should we get rid of our unprofitable customers?
10. Maybe we should hire contractors instead of employees?
11. I think it is time to cut health insurance benefits.
12. We could stop making 401(k) matches for now.

13. Maybe I will go without a check until things get better?
14. I'll stop putting money towards my kids' college for now.
15. We should cancel employee bonuses.
16. I'll just start furloughing employees.
17. We could stop advertising to save some money.
18. Let's put that store remodel on hold.
19. We'll reduce our insurance costs.
20. We'll automate our customer service.

There is a common problem with all these thoughts…

Each one is a defensive reaction that SEEMS like a logical decision. But, in truth, choosing these actions can be very dangerous for the long-run.

Here are some examples of how these seemingly cautious decisions could be disastrous to your business

Example 1:

Your Action: You decide to cut employee bonuses.

Short-Term Result: You reduce your payroll costs and increase your cash flow

Long-Term Result: Your high-performing team members are highly motivated by your compensation plan which includes their merit-based bonuses. Your low-performing employees don't care because they never get a good bonus anyway. So, your high-performing people quit and go to the competition, you are left with your low-performing employees, and your business is in jeopardy.

Example 2:

Your Action: You decide to reduce your evening store hours.

Short-Term Result: You reduce your payroll costs and utility costs and increase your cash flow.

Long-Term Result: You didn't consider that more people are working from home now, so they are visiting more local stores than ever before and shopping later at night. By shortening your hours, you've made it difficult for your regular customers to shop with you so they decide to buy online or go to a local competitor who's still open. Once the relationship is severed, they never come back to your store and your business is in jeopardy.

Example 3:

Your Action: You decide to stop all advertising.

Short-Term Result: Your advertising costs decrease and you increase your cash flow.

Long-Term Result: You didn't measure the effectiveness of your Google AdWords or Facebook campaigns so you didn't realize that over 60% of your online sales and inquiries were coming from these campaigns. Your revenues plummet. Your competitors increase their advertising budget and your business is in jeopardy.

Example 4:

Your Action: You furlough all employees for 4 weeks over the next 4 months.

Short-Term Result: You reduce your payroll costs and increase cash flow.

Long-Term Result: The best employees can always find a job somewhere. So, your furloughed employees talk to your competitors, who are still actively recruiting as well as offering a signing bonus and one extra week of vacation. You lose your best employees and your business is in jeopardy.

Example 5:

Your Action: You discount your prices.

Short-Term Result: Your revenue increases based on a higher volume.

Long-Term Result: Your main supplier goes out of business and only one other supplier is available. The remaining supplier has much higher costs than your previous supplier. In fact, each time you sell a product you lose money and your business is in jeopardy.

We could go on and on...The common theme is that small businesses need to be very careful not to make knee jerk decisions that could help us in the short-term but be fatal to our businesses in the long-term.

Restart Insight: *Consider the long-term implications of short-term decisions.*

Interview: Jim Lindenberg, The Union House

Jim Lindenberg is a classic serial entrepreneur. He has owned many different types of businesses, is always seeking to help other business owners succeed, and is a regular investor in small businesses. Jim and his 11 businesses have won over 35 awards. He has owned and was the CEO of World Class Wire and Cable, World Class Health and Fitness, The Milwaukee Wave, Wave of Hope, Velocity Sports, NX Level Sports Performance, Legends of the Field, and Master Z's.

Jim currently owns and is the CEO of Lindy Enterprises (small business consulting), JML Holdings (property management), and recently purchased a historical fine dining restaurant named The Union House in Genesee Depot (west of Milwaukee). For this new venture, Jim is applying his refined small business growth strategies to make the restaurant thrive.

Here are Jim's thoughts on growing The Union House during this crisis:

"I have always been a glass is half full person. Don't ever give up. Whenever someone says something can't be done, when things are down, I look for opportunities. Shortly after I purchased The Union House Restaurant, I had to close temporarily it due to the regulations from the Coronavirus. I just asked myself how can we take advantage of this downtime to grow the business? So, we did a complete remodel of the restaurant (inside and outside), we overhauled the website and developed a new logo, we retrained our employees, and we redid our kitchen. We developed personalized meals, family meals, and added new items to our menu for curbside pick-up and offered local delivery. Other restaurants closed and just cut employees and costs....those restaurants will have a harder time reopening and may not make it. The Union House growth and reputation are now going to accelerate like never before."

Brainstorming New Options for Your Small Business

So, how can you develop new options? It's time to brainstorm!

If you are not familiar with brainstorming the key principles are as follows:

1. Generate as many new ideas as possible.

2. Generate ideas from as many people as possible. Especially those outside of your company.

3. **Do not criticize any ideas.** Even people seasoned in brainstorming immediately fall into criticizing ideas as they come up. My favorite being, "we did that XX years ago and it didn't work." If you want to really drive the point home, repeat "Do not criticize any ideas." for every other "step" (2, 4, 6…)

4. Have someone else facilitate, if possible.

5. Review the ideas based on the short-term results and long-term results

    I recommend that you get someone outside of your organization who understands your type of business. They should have experience facilitating brainstorming sessions.

    If you don't have the luxury of time or money to conduct a facilitated brainstorming session, simply follow these steps using your board of directors, owners, key staff members, or simply volunteers who understand your business, such as mentors:

    Brainstorming Session Instructions:

    1. Hold a meeting away from your place of business but at a location without distractions (e.g. private back room at a local restaurant). Set

aside up to 45 minutes per brainstorming topic. Some topics might take as little as 10 minutes and some up to 45 minutes. The average brainstorming session typically takes about 30 minutes.

2. Have someone with neat handwriting take notes.

3. Purchase a large pad of flip chart paper (I like the flip charts with the adhesive on the back so you can stick the paper on the wall).

4. Purchase a set of different colored markers.

5. Put a bowl of candy or snacks in the middle of the table(s).

6. Put some stress balls or other items in the middle of the table(s). This helps those people that are kinesthetic learners (learn by doing) and those that have issues paying attention.

7. Turn on some relaxing music (this helps lower the stress of people attending the meeting).

8. Assemble the people who are going to participate and, if possible, get your board of directors or the owners in a room.

9. Turn off all smartphones and laptops.

10. Explain the following:

    a. You will be conducting a brainstorming session to help determine the future of the company.
    b. No ideas are bad ideas. [YOU MUST NOT CRITICIZE ANY IDEAS OR THIS ENTIRE EXERCISE FALLS APART]

c. You will be spending the next hour exploring new ideas to help the company thrive. You are not just looking to survive by cutting costs(although those can be options too). You are looking for ways to GROW the company.
d. Ask the following questions and have your notetaker write down the answers on the flip chart paper each question must have a different sheet:
   i. What are the biggest challenges we are facing? This can be a therapeutic way to let people vent. **Don't let this go on more than 10 minutes.** It will simply drag people down and it will impede the ability to generate new, creative, powerful ideas for the business.
   ii. What are the company's biggest strengths?
   iii. What are the biggest opportunities we have?
   iv. Describe our best customers.
   v. Describe our worst customers (yes, there is such a thing as a bad customer).
   vi. Describe the best products/services that we offer.
   vii. Describe our worst products/services that we offer.
   viii. If money and time were no object what new products/services would we offer?

11. Thank everyone for their time and input.

12. Have a meal or drinks to reduce the stress of the exercise

Now, in separate meetings, review the notes with all the critical decision-makers in your business, and consider your findings. It is important to have all the critical decision-makers in the same meeting. One decision that is made in one functional area of your business could have an impact on another area of your business. For example, a meeting with customer service could impact engineering, finance, and sales. It's important to keep an open mind and be willing to consider all the ideas presented and the way that they would function together.

Important learning here: Nokia used to make rubber military boots and eventually ended up in the cellular phone business (before getting purchased by Microsoft). How did they do it? They kept an open mind to new business opportunities, kept the employees that could best adapt to the new business model, hired experts to help make the transition, conducted research to analyze the market, assessed the findings from talking to customers to identify opportunities that capitalized on the new company's strengths and launched a completely different company.

If Nokia can go from rubber military boots to making cellular phones your company can probably make less severe changes and reap the success that comes with adaptation.

Interview: Henry Schwartz, Mobcraft Beer

Henry Schwartz launched his crowdsourced brewing company, Mobcraft Beer, while still in college. Henry realized that even though you had to be 21-years-old to buy beer, you did not have to be 21 to buy beer ingredients. He started asking his college friends for ideas on recipes and eventually took that model online. Henry eventually pitched on ABC's Shark Tank and has raised millions in startup capital. He now has his own brewery, wholesale beer business, and still operates his crowdsourced beer service.

Henry spoke about how Mobcraft generated new product ideas by brainstorming with his team.

"When the Coronavirus happened, it decimated our taproom business and draft beer sales. People were still purchasing our products in retail and online but we needed to figure out a way to make up the revenue lost from our taproom. We had to do something quickly to help cover our overhead and anything was on the table. So, our staff brainstormed other ways to market Mobcraft Beer to capitalize on the fact that our customers were staying in the homes and that they still wanted experiences [not to just buy beer]. We pulled from all the enjoyable experiences we have had with beer in the past to create some very fun and well attended virtual events.

We started hosting Zoom events with customers based on rotating kits of beer + "things that go well with beer" we now have beer and ice cream pairings, beer and popcorn pairings, we've done IPA Home School, Sushi and beer dinner, and even an online flip cup tournament! This helped drive home Mobcraft as an experience for beer lovers not just a source of beer like every other brewer. Our clients stop by the brewery and pick-up kits, purchase apparel, sign-up for our newsletter, engage in our social media presence. So, we are not just generating immediate revenue from the pairing kits but growing long-term relationships and more long-lasting emotional connections with fans than we have before.

To decide which of your new, brainstormed ideas are worth following, you have to thoroughly understand your competition. So, let's take a look at how to analyze what, or who, you're up against.

Analyzing the Competition

One of the easiest and best methods for analyzing how your business stacks up against the competition is the SWOT Analysis.

SWOT stands for Strengths, Weaknesses, Opportunities, and Threats. Going through this simple exercise will provide you with deep insight into how your business operates. It can show you how many "macro" things, such as politics, demographics, competition, the law, and more affect your business. Additionally, you'll learn about the effect on your business of "micro" factors such as customers, employees, distribution channels and suppliers, direct competitors, investors, media, and the general public.

Once completed, you'll understand your small business better than you ever have before – with a clear picture of its standing in your market and against your competition.

When creating your SWOT, consider the following:

Small Business Idea "Strengths": What strengths does your small business currently have relative to your competitors? Focus on sustainable competitive advantages, not just an advantage you may currently have. For example, avoid falling into the classic trap of saying, "we are cheaper." Being lower-priced is easy when you are a small organization with no overhead, but as your costs increase, your margins will decrease and you will lose your "competitive strength."

Small Business Idea "Weaknesses": Identify weaknesses in your business model that will be difficult to overcome, at least initially. Avoid falling into the classic trap of saying, "we have no weaknesses." Every business has some weaknesses. Take the time to identify areas that could create issues for your business now or in the future. Once the weaknesses are identified, you can try to minimize those weaknesses as you roll out and scale your business.

Small Business Idea "Opportunities": What opportunities exist in the market – problems that your business can solve or unmet needs that your business can fill? Ideally, these are opportunities that your competitors have not yet identified or do not have the capability to meet. The opportunity drives your value proposition. Think about the long-term as well as short-term opportunities. Perhaps look for changes in laws that could assist you, growth of new sectors in the economy, competitors that might go out of business, etc.

Small Business Idea "Threats": What threats will you face in the short and long term that could significantly diminish your capacity to grow or could potentially put you out of business? The threats could come from competitors, access to capital, changes in the economy, environmental factors, not being able to find cost-effective staff, a limited number of suppliers, technology changes, etc.

Create your SWOT using this grid (this is best done on a whiteboard with your team and an objective outside facilitator).

Strengths	Weaknesses
Opportunities	Threats

If you would like to take an even deeper look at your business and explore additional ways to develop future business models, I recommend using **Porter's Five Forces Model.**

Porter's Five Forces Model was developed by Michael Porter from Harvard University. This exercise helps define the sources of competition at a more microenvironmental level. The focus is on five forces that determine the competitive intensity and, therefore, the attractiveness (or lack of it) of an industry in terms of its profitability.

Porter's Five Forces is a powerful tool that requires some heavy lifting. If you have the time and wish to tackle it, the benefits are very valuable.

We mustn't just stand still as small businesses. To THRIVE we need to think creatively, look for new opportunities, and reevaluate our business models from top to bottom.

Go into this next section with an open mind. Have you ever considered these fallacies to be true of your business or idea?

1) We know everything our customers want.
2) Our customers love all of our products and services.

3) Our customers are loyal and would never use a competitor.
4) Our customers would never buy online.
5) We have amazing customer service.
6) Our marketing is cost-effectively driving sales.
7) Our team members are exactly who we need now and for the future.
8) We will never take outside funding for our company.
9) We don't need any patents, copyrights, or trademarks.
10) We must ship all of our products ourselves.
11) We will never use Amazon, they are our biggest competitor.
12) Our software is working fine. We don't need anything else.
13) We don't need to invest any money in our business.
14) We don't need a succession plan for our company.
15) Our competitors aren't going to change.
16) My employees would never go and work for the competition.
17) There is nothing I can learn from small businesses.
18) Our salespeople always achieve their best.
19) We don't need to use distributors or agents.
20) Our website is fine.
21) Social media won't help our business.
22) Our suppliers are the best available.
23) We would never take an outside investment in our company.
24) We don't need any new board members.
25) Our cash flow is strong.

If you've ever had any of these thoughts, you aren't alone. It's easy to fall into the trap of assuming that everything is great – especially if you've had some success. BUT…

If you want your small business to THRIVE, especially during times of chaos, you need to be willing to be critical of every aspect of your business and open to developing a new business model.

1. Be willing to take the time to find out what is going on in the market.
2. Talk to your current customers and talk about prospective customers.
3. Do competitive research.
4. Talk with new, potential suppliers.
5. Talk with your team members but also talk to potential, new team members.
6. Analyze potential, new products, and services.

Yes, this is going to take work. If it seems like too much, find team members or mentors who can help. But you must lead this process.

Interview: Aaron Jagdfeld, CEO, Generac

Aaron Jagdfeld is the President and CEO of Generac. Aaron began his career as an accountant at Deloitte. Then he joined Generac as an accountant and rose through the ranks to Corporate Controller, Chief Financial Officer, and then into his current role as President and CEO. Aaron led the company through the economic crisis of 2008, ownership changes, natural disasters, and more. Aaron was the perfect person to share his insights on creating an adaptable business model.

"Generac began in the 1950s as a manufacturer of portable generators. By the late 1990s, we eventually sold our portable products division which was a major portion of the business to private equity who ultimately sold it to Briggs and Stratton a few years after that. We decided to retain our stationary products business including residential home standby generators which were a very small piece of business for us at the time. These stationery products were sold primarily to businesses through traditional industrial two-step dealer channels. We weren't selling or marketing to consumers at all at that point, we had seen an opportunity here even though we didn't know exactly how big the opportunity was going to be we hadn't established any channels strategy, any
direct marketing strategy, or any of the operations needed to bring a product like this successfully to market.

Eventually, we launched the home standby generator category based on a three-pronged approach:

*First, we looked at **Awareness**: We needed to educate homeowners that a more sophisticated way of solving their power availability problems even existed.*

*Next, we looked at **Affordability**: We looked at the total cost of ownership. It is one thing for a manufacturer to make the product itself affordable. It is an entirely different thing to consider the entire cost of ownership for the consumer. We looked at not just* the cost of the product, but the cost of installation, the cost of delivery, the cost of maintenance...the entire cost of ownership.

Lastly, we looked at **Availability:** We needed to consider the importance of making the product widely accessible and we decided the best way to do that was through an omnichannel strategy. We thought about the way the consumer wanted to buy, not the way that was easiest to sell. Some customers might want a "turn-key" solution through one of our electrical contractor dealers, some might want to manage the project themselves and purchase through Home Depot, Lowe's, or even online. Fundamentally, we asked ourselves... Who are we to dictate the way that the consumer wants to buy'

The following graphic demonstrates a method used by Generac to analyze the Demand Creation Process (created by Harvard Business School). Mapping out a similar process for your small business can help you identify areas that could refine your business model.

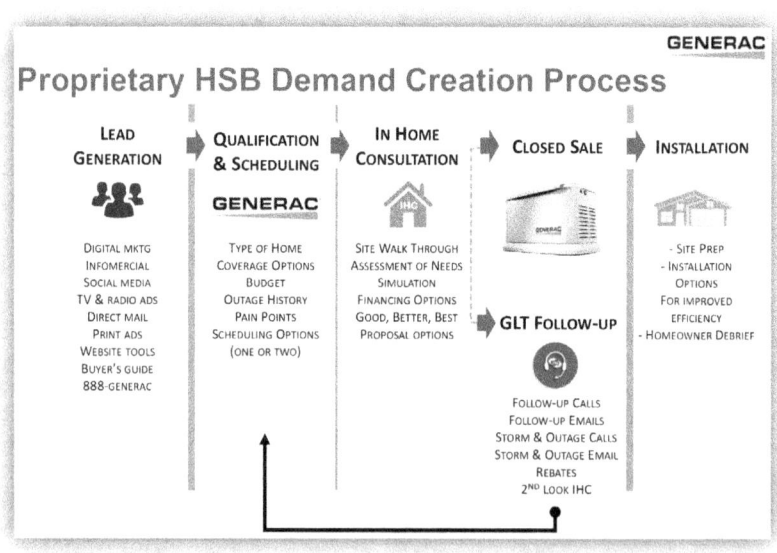

Source: 2020, Generac Annual Report, February 13, 2020

Interview: Frank Siebrecht, SCORE

Frank Siebrecht spent a great deal of his career as a VP of Client Planning Research at Bader Rutter a B2B (Business-to-Business) advertising agency and I was fortunate enough to have him as my first small business mentor in his role as a consultant at SCORE. SCORE is a resource partner of the U.S. Small Business Administration (SBA), SCORE has helped more than 11 million entrepreneurs through mentoring, workshops, and educational resources since 1964.

I asked Frank to discuss his insights on looking beyond your existing customer base when operating during chaotic times.

*"Dave, some small businesses won't do anything differently after a crisis, these companies end-up in really bad shape. Others will talk with their customers and make tweaks to their business. But the best will not just talk with their customers but take the time to talk with their competitors' customers. Whether it is retail, insurance, hospitality, manufacturing, medical, tech, or any other kind of business it doesn't matter, the clever companies take the time to do this research. Not only do they do research online but they locate their competitor's customers and have in-depth conversations. But you can't just ask what don't you like about your current provider but what do you like, what would you change. You need to understand not just what they need but what they want. Their **needs** might be being satisfied but there could be many wants that are not getting fulfilled that is where the real opportunity exists. You might need to offer new products and services or perhaps you need to do a better job of marketing your current products and services you have that meet their wants not just their needs."*

Market Discovery – Go Get the Truth

New business models' ideas can be personal, especially if you have spent a great deal of time generating the idea and are contemplating dedicating a career to the small business idea. You may try to avoid people that could give you news you don't want to hear, but that aversion can also doom your small business ideas. It's important to go out and seek the truth.

One of my favorite movies of all time is, *A Few Good Men*. The film is a military drama with a final intense courtroom scene between Tom Cruise and Jack Nicholson. During the final courtroom scene, where Jack Nicholson is getting grilled on the stand by Tom Cruise, he yells from the top of his lungs…

"You can't handle the truth!"

You, too, need to "find the truth" about whether you have a viable idea. So, get out of your office, store or home, and talk to people who might buy your product or service if it was available to them. It might seem scary at first but you will eventually find out that this is quite fun…if you take it as an opportunity to learn, to meet new people and perhaps even to find future customers. Avoid getting defensive, although this can be difficult because our small businesses are very personal to us. Criticisms of our business ideas can often be mistaken as personal criticism because they're our ideas and we think they're great – but they're not personal. The person giving feedback doesn't know who came up with the idea or that you are particularly attached to the idea. Try to stay objective. Relentlessly moving forward, learning, and refining your ideas and business model.

You, and possibly your team members, will eventually master the skill of going out and conducting market discovery!

It's important to note that asking friends, family members, and your current team if they like your idea and how much they would pay for the idea is **not** a sound marketing research strategy. In fact, it is probably a recipe for disaster. Friends and family, in general, are an easy source for feedback, but they are not a representative sample of prospective customers. Talking to team members is definitely important. However, current team members can sometimes have blinders on as to what is going on in the marketplace, or they might not want to share ideas if that could negatively impact their job.

Spend a significant amount of time talking to a random sample of real prospective customers, with whom you have no relationship, to get the cold hard truth about your idea. Talk with people you don't know. Talk with potential buyers living throughout the country or the world (thank goodness for the internet!).

Restart Insight: *Share your idea with as many current and prospective **paying** customers as you can to refine your small business ideas and create new business model opportunities.*

Market Discovery Questions

Next, we need to create questions for our market discovery. A helpful tool when creating these questions is using a Solution Map. As you can see below, we are focused on the area between the customer's current situation and the ideal situation. We are trying to solve the pain point with our solution (idea).

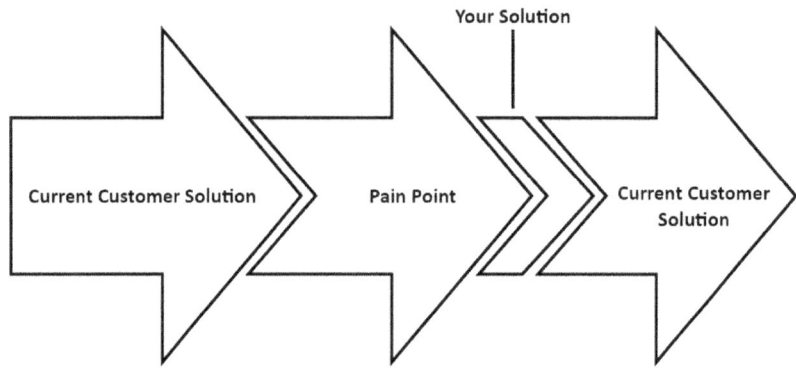

Initial Hypotheses

When we begin with our idea, we have many hypotheses (theories about our idea). However, we can't presume that our hypotheses are reality. We need to spend the time to validate these hypotheses or we risk wasting an incredible amount of time and money.

Let's say we had a small business idea for an electricity-saving service connected to a mobile application. Here are some of our possible hypotheses:

1. Consumers feel they spend too much on electricity.
2. Consumers do not have an easy way to monitor their electricity consumption.
3. Consumers would like a mobile app where they can monitor their electricity consumption in real-time.
4. Consumers would be willing to pay $4.99 for the app download and $2.99/month.

5. We should launch the app first in the App Store.
6. Consumers would primarily like to learn about us through their electric company.
7. The electric company would like to promote our mobile app to help reduce customer calls when customer bills arrive.
8. The electric company will want to "white label" our mobile app.
9. Our cost to develop our mobile app will be under $25k.
10. Our cost to develop the hardware to integrate with home thermostats will be under $50k.
11. Our installation will be provided by certified electricians throughout the U.S.
12. Our first pilot markets should be New York and Boston.
13. We will be able to patent our technology.
14. Our first-year operating budget will be under $150,000.

Discovery Questions

Before we jump into specific market discovery questions to test our hypotheses, let's review the two forms of questions and the benefits of using each question.

> **Open-ended questions** – Open-ended questions are questions used to elicit an open, free response. Open-ended questions yield a great deal of information. We want to focus our discovery interviews on open-ended questions, especially at the beginning of the discovery interview. Not only does starting with the discovery meeting help us get a big picture of their current situation at the beginning, but it also helps get the prospective customer to open up to us.

Open-ended questions begin with words such as:

- What
- Why
- Will
- How
- Where
- Describe
- Tell

Closed-ended questions – Closed-ended questions are questions used to refine an understanding of the situation. Closed-ended questions typically yield brief answers such as a yes or no, or other specific responses. These questions should be answered later in the discovery interview.

Closed-ended questions begin with words such as:

- Do
- Can
- Where
- Does
- Did
- Could
- Should
- Is
- Are
- Have

Market discovery interviews are a blend of both open-ended and closed-ended questions. A helpful process to use when conducting discovery research is a method called the **funnel approach**. The concept behind the funnel approach is that you get the most comprehensive information when you ask a combination of open- and closed-ended questions, in that order. The quick pointer here: This is also the best method to use when finding out customers' needs when you are ready to begin selling your product or service.

FUNNEL APPROACH

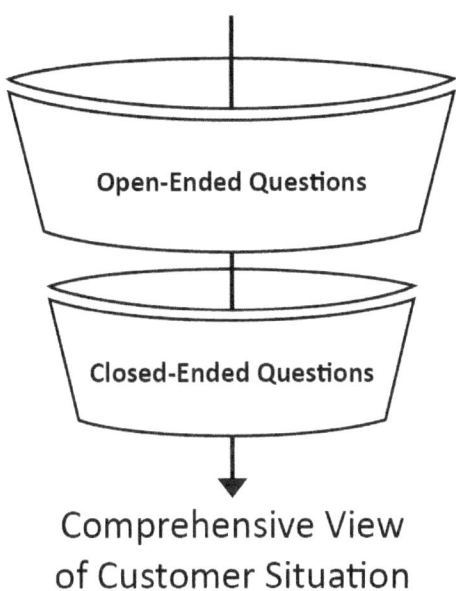

You might be tempted to send email surveys to conduct initial discovery research. This is a bad idea for several reasons. You need to capture a wide variety of information from these people. Utilizing electronic surveys means you are essentially using closed-ended questions, which prevent you from gathering the range of information you need. Additionally, closed-ended questions often tend to be leading questions, which defeats the purpose of getting honest responses from your participants.

If you cannot meet with potential customers face-to-face, you might try via webinar or video chat. This allows you an opportunity to read body language and provides other benefits, such as gaining insights from the customer's environment too. You can use a basic service such as Skype or Zoom. Keep in mind, if you have prospective customers who are going to be spending a great deal of money with you (e.g. a B2B client), spend the money for the professional webinar service such as WebEx. Making a great first impression with these people is critical.

Restart Insight: *Don't just ask leading questions when conducting discovery. Ask the questions that will validate or invalidate your hypotheses by using open- and closed-ended questions. These are the questions that will help increase your success.*

Resist the temptation to share your solution (small business idea) in the discovery interview until you are comfortable that you have a comprehensive view of the customer's current situation. If you share it too early, you will simply bias people's answers and make false assumptions that could be fatal to your small business.

Here are some examples of the most critical customer situational questions you need to ask:

Customer Situational Questions

1. Describe your current situation relative to _____.
2. What is currently working well for you?
3. What challenges or problems are you facing?
4. What solutions are you using to solve those problems?
5. Where did you find out about those solutions?
6. How well are those solutions working for you?
7. Are you aware of any other solutions?
8. Why have you not looked at other solutions?
9. How much do you pay for the current solution?
10. How do you feel about the amount you are paying?
11. What would the ideal solution look like to you?
12. Would you be willing to consider a new solution?
13. Where would you most likely learn about the new solution?
14. What would convince you that the new solution would fix the problem?

Write down a few customer situational questions for your Small business idea here:

1.

2.

3.

4.

5.

6.

7.

8.

9.

10.

Solution-Specific Questions

Once you have completed your customer situation-specific questions, you can present your solution and then start asking solution-specific questions. Avoid pitching them on why they should select your solution. I know that this is very difficult to do, given that you likely have an emotional connection to your small business idea. Here are sample questions you could ask:

1. What do you think of _____ (your solution)?
2. What do you specifically like about the solution?
3. What do you dislike about the solution?
4. What would you change about the solution?
5. Where would you most likely learn about this solution?
6. What specific sources would you trust to validate that this solution would work?
7. Would you purchase this solution?
8. Where would you want to purchase this solution?
9. How frequently would you purchase this solution?
10. How much would you pay for the solution?
11. Would you be willing to pre-pay for the solution?
12. What payment terms (e.g. net 30) would you be willing to accept?
13. Would you expect any specific warranties or guarantees? If yes, tell me about what those warranties or guarantees would look like.
14. Would you like to participate in our pilot (if at this point you think you could generate substantial information from this prospective customer)?

Write down some of your Solution-Specific questions:

1.

2.

3.

4.

5.

6.

7.

8.

9.

10.

How many discovery questions should you ask?

I frequently get asked this question from entrepreneurs and small businesses, "Gee, how many people should I talk to know if people want my product?" I will give you my academic answer first. "You should use a representative sample size of your population of customers." If you haven't taken a statistics class, a representative sample size is the number of people, organizations, etc. that you need to talk to in order to draw a reliable conclusion. You can use tools such as sample size calculators to determine a "representative sample size." Use a Sample Size Calculator Tool, easily found on Google.

It's okay to "Take It Out Back".

Researching by asking discovery questions will help you refine your small business idea. Frankly, it might make you reconsider even proceeding with your idea.

Killing an idea, or "taking it out back" (Old Yeller movie reference here – watch the movie if you haven't seen it. Spoiler alert it has a very sad ending!) as I refer to the process, is a much better decision than dedicating years of your life and countless amounts of money to an idea that is destined for failure. Frankly, it is the humane thing to do.

So, yes, it's okay to take an idea "out back." You will naturally feel deflated; it can feel very personal. However, small business owners don't usually develop one idea and then stop. Usually, ideas will start emanating from their creative minds shortly after they decide not to pursue a particular small business idea.

I have had over 20 business ideas on my smartphone at all times. I simply put them in the Notes app of my iPhone and come back to them if I think it has a true market opportunity. Then I go out and talk to prospective customers to see if there is indeed a pain point, how they are solving the problem and what they think of my solution.

If you have never taken the time to reevaluate your business model or truly generate new small business ideas you might only have one idea, but over time you will generate many others. Some will be derived from your first small business idea but others could be a completely different business model. Exercising this creative part of your brain will make it more productive. Of course, during your discovery, you might find that your business model is not sustainable but it is better to find out early, pivot your business model, sell or shut-down the business than continue down a path that is proven to not be viable.

Restart Insight: *You might find during your discovery that your business model is no longer sustainable. It is better to find out now, pivot your business model, sell or shut-down the business than continue down a path that is no longer viable and create years of stress, aggravation, and losing money.*

Determining your Market Size

Once you have gotten to the point where you are comfortable your solution (your new small business ideas) addresses a real pain point, we need to determine the market size.
Simply said, is the market big enough to justify the money and time invested?

Before we move on, it is important to understand some more terminology to help identify our market opportunity.

Total Addressable Market (TAM) – Total number of customers in a particular market.

Serviceable Addressable Market (SAM) – Segment of the TAM that is targeted by your products/services.

Serviceable Obtainable Market (SOM) – Portion of the SAM that you can realistically capture.

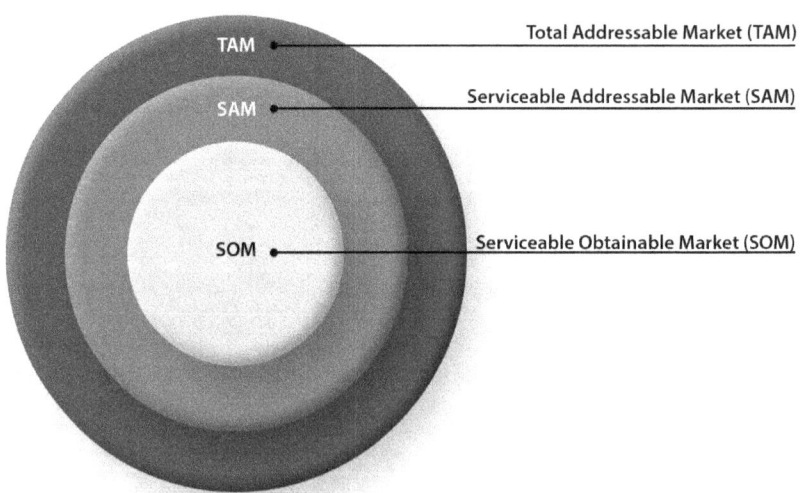

For the sake of illustration, I am going to create a fictional small business idea. This small business idea will be used to demonstrate analyzing the TAM, SAM, and SOM. We will also use this same example for the upcoming chapters on developing your brand and marketing.

Small Business Idea: Let's say you have a small business idea that is comprised of software to coordinate residential care for seniors. You might scope out the market in the following manner:

1. **The Total Addressable Market (TAM)** – There are currently 8,350,100 people in the U.S. who receive support from the five main long-term care services; home health agencies (4,742,500), nursing homes (1,383,700), hospices (1,244,500), residential care communities (713,300) and adult daycare service centers (273,200).

2. **The Serviceable Addressable Market (SAM)** – Our software is targeted at those providing home health care. Therefore, our SAM is 4,742,500 people.

3. **Serviceable Obtainable Market (SOM)** – Perhaps we estimate that we can capture 1 percent of the market in the first three years. Therefore, the SOM would be 47,425 (1% x 4,742,500) people.

Data Source: Family Caregiver Alliance, Feb 2015

Restart Insight: *You need to be very careful in estimating the Serviceable Obtainable Market. The SOM can be used to show you have a grasp on market size, but it is important to be very conservative when estimating this number, especially if you decide to meet with prospective investors or pitch accelerators.*

Developing a Sustainable Business Model

Business models describe the methods that a business uses to create and deliver value to its customers. Taking the time to develop your initial business model can be critical to the life of your small business. Your business will evolve over time and as you "pivot" (change elements within your business model).

Traditional Business Model Elements include:
- Value proposition
- Customer segments
- Revenue models
- Marketing and sales
- Business partner relationships
- Cost structure

To make the development of a business model more comprehensive, Alexander Osterwalder developed a graphical tool that helps small businesses considerably. This tool is called the Business Model Canvas (BMC). This tool is not only well-respected at institutions including Stanford, MIT, and the University of Chicago, but is almost universally embraced by angel investors, entrepreneurs, and innovative small businesses. I require that my student entrepreneurs use the BMC to develop an initial foundation for their business. It is a very helpful tool to help them guide their discovery.

You can watch a video demonstrating how the Business Model Canvas works by visiting this website: http://bit.ly/2i4bWDs

The Business Model Canvas includes nine key elements you need to define and refine as you move through the discovery process.

1. Value propositions
2. Customer segments
3. Customer relationships
4. Distribution channels
5. Key resources
6. Key activities
7. Key partners
8. Cost structure
9. Revenue streams

The Business Model Canvas

Source: Osterwalder A, Pigneur Y, Business Model Generation, 2010

When developing your Business Model Canvas, the questions that need to be answered for each of the nine elements include (but are not limited to):

1. Customer Segments
   a. List all of your various customer segments (initial customer types and future types).
   b. I recommend including users in here as well—those who use your product but do not pay you.

2. Customer Relationships
   a. How are you going to interact with your customers?
   b. Where are some of your initial sources of prospects?
   c. How will you make the initial sale?
   d. What methods will you use to provide customer support?

3. Value Proposition
   a. What value does your business provide the customer?
   b. What is the customer problem you are solving?

c. Is there a sustainable competitive advantage?
   d. How are you delivering the service?

4. Distribution (Sales) Channels
   a. What sales channels will you use?
   b. Which sales channels should you use first?
   c. Which sales channels are the most effective?
   d. Which sales channels are the most efficient?

5. Revenue Streams
   a. How much are customers willing to pay you (based on your discovery)?
   b. What methods do they want to use to pay you?
   c. How frequently do they want to pay you?
   d. Describe all of the potential revenue streams (note: only having one revenue stream is a recipe for disaster – think of multiple options).

6. Key Activities
   a. Do you need to secure a patent?
   b. Should you hire a software engineer as an independent contractor?
   c. Do you need warehouse space?
   d. When should you rent an office space?

7. Key Resources
   a. What are the critical elements of your small business's success?
   b. How many people do you need on your core development team?
   c. Should you use direct or indirect sales channels?
   d. How many delivery trucks do you need?

8. Key Partners
   a. What is your priority market? Example: West Coast, Midwest, and East Coast distributors.
   b. Who should you select for your law firm?
   c. Who should you select for your software development firm?

9. Cost Structure
   a. What is your target cost of goods sold?
   b. What is your cost of customer acquisition?
   c. What will be your initial capital costs?

Business Model Canvas Tools

With Canvas tools you create some order in all the chaos and unknown. A Business Model Canvas outlines nine critical elements giving the small business a logical discovery roadmap toward a viable business model. You first discover and validate significant problems for customers, and then you can validate the unique value your business offers. With Canvas tools and the use of the Lean Small Business methodology, there is a bit of a process to follow, making business model development more accessible and less mysterious.

Here are two, FREE web-based tools that I recommend for small businesses to develop new business models with the Business Model Canvas.

Canvanizer - canvanizer.com

Strategyzer - strategyzer.com

Step 2 – Marketing Your Small Business

As you change your business model, create new business ideas, launch new products and services, open new locations or simply decide you want to grow revenue, you may find that you need to evaluate your brand and focus on impactful, measurable marketing.

What is a Brand?

You can find many definitions of a brand, but one I feel most efficiently and effectively captures the essence of a brand is the following:

Brand: A brand is a promise that a company, product, or service will provide to its customers. The brand is how you represent your customer value proposition.

Interview: Jerry David, Prescient Financial Solutions

For insights about brand promises, I visited with Jerry David. Jerry is the Founder and CEO of Prescient Financial Solutions. Prescient is one of the top financial planning firms associated with Northwestern Mutual. The Financial Times has recognized Prescient as one of the **Top Wealth Management Companies in the U.S.**

Jerry shared his thoughts about the importance of providing communications and accessibility to clients during times of crisis.

"I began my career actually as an engineer and that carried through to my business, Prescient. Prescient was initially founded on the premise that we create custom-engineered financial solutions, not cookie-cutter financial products and services. Every client has different needs and so that is how we built our business. We still focus on custom-engineered financial solutions but we are much more than that.

We pride ourselves in helping our clients live the life they desire.

When our company faced a time of crisis, I think back to 2008. Communicating with clients proactively is critical during times of chaos. If a potential client is with the competitor and they come to us they will usually tell us they don't hear from their advisor very often. This is so important when the market is down and they are concerned. But they shouldn't have to contact their financial advisor to find out what is going on. When you experience turbulence on a plane you don't ask the pilot what is going on. The pilot tells you what is happening and why it is happening.

I have a perfect example. I have a client who, in 2008, had **$2.5 million** in assets with us. The crash happened and we didn't contact him. As the crash was occurring he emailed me directly and said, **"Jerry how much would it cost me to move my money somewhere else?"** I was naturally very concerned and asked why he wanted to move his money. He responded, "Jerry when significant losses or gains occur I don't expect you to always be able to tell me why these swings are happening but I do expect you to call me with anything you know."

Needless to say, it was a great lesson for me and my entire team on the importance of communication. Now that client invites me to his homes, we go on vacations together, we are connected in every aspect of the word. Small businesses have the advantage of being nimble and they need to capitalize on that advantage during times of chaos by communicating openly with their clients with as much reliable information to their clients as possible.

I think the other important lesson for small businesses is accessibility. You always need to be available to your clients. It doesn't matter what kind of business you are in. Your clients should be able to contact you. During the COVID 19 outbreak, our office was closed for 8 weeks. So, I made sure that we set-up all of our advisors at home and made it a seamless transition for our clients. Our clients got the same personal touch as if they were contacting us at our office. Just because a business is facing some kind of crisis it doesn't mean that their customers don't still need their help, their *products, and their services, you just have to figure out a different way of delivering from the normal method."*

Within the area of marketing, developing your brand can be one of the most enjoyable, but also one of the most maddening processes. It is critical to take the time to consider your brand through your customer's eyes first and not your own. Use words that make it clear what your product or service provides. You might have brand names for various products and services. For now, we are going to focus on creating a brand name for your small business itself.

Avoid the Brand Name Boat Anchor

The Sexy vs. Specific Scale

I have found that some small businesses when branding or rebranding their company or creating new products and services, gravitate toward creating a brand name that is sexy, exciting, and that they "perceive" to be memorable. When I am meeting with entrepreneurs and small businesses I grab my dry erase marker, head to the whiteboard and write the following;

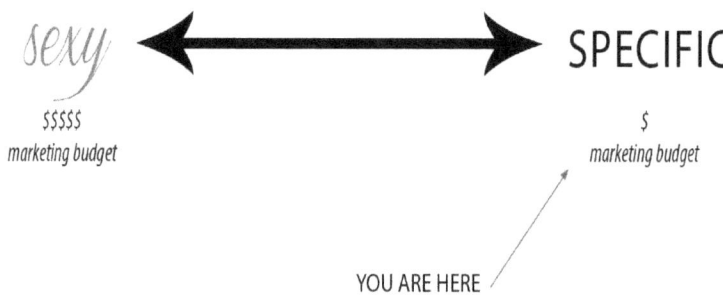

The temptation when creating the brand name for your idea is to create some **"Sexy."** However, when your marketing budget is small or $0 you don't have the luxury of a brand that is sexy. Instead, you need to quickly convey what your brand is and the product/service of the brand. If you don't your brand is going to get lost in the hundreds or thousands of other brands that people see every day. You need to focus on **"Specific"** and not "Sexy."

Now, there are exceptions to this rule. For example, if your brand is complementing other products that you own, you can quickly explain the product in a tagline or other value proposition, etc.

One of the main considerations I see small business people overlooking is the impact that their brand name has on search engine optimization (SEO). SEO is the proactive process you go through to increase your page rank by using organic or "free" methods (not paid advertisements). Page rank is the position a website occupies on a search engine (e.g. Second place down on a search within Google) relative to other websites. Think about the specific words (aka keywords) customers will type into a search engine if they are looking for a product/service such as yours.

For example, if we type "hats" in the search box within Google, the screen shown in the graphic below pops up. Notice that the third actual search result (not paid ads—the images on top and the first search result "Lids") is for hats.com. That is about the least sexy brand name you can imagine. But you will notice they are on the first page of Google. In fact, they appear within the first three spots (which is important) ... without spending any money. I am not saying you should not spend money on paid search advertising; it can be very cost-effective. But, why spend money you don't have just to increase your visibility in search engines when you could be spending that money in other ways to launch and grow your small business?

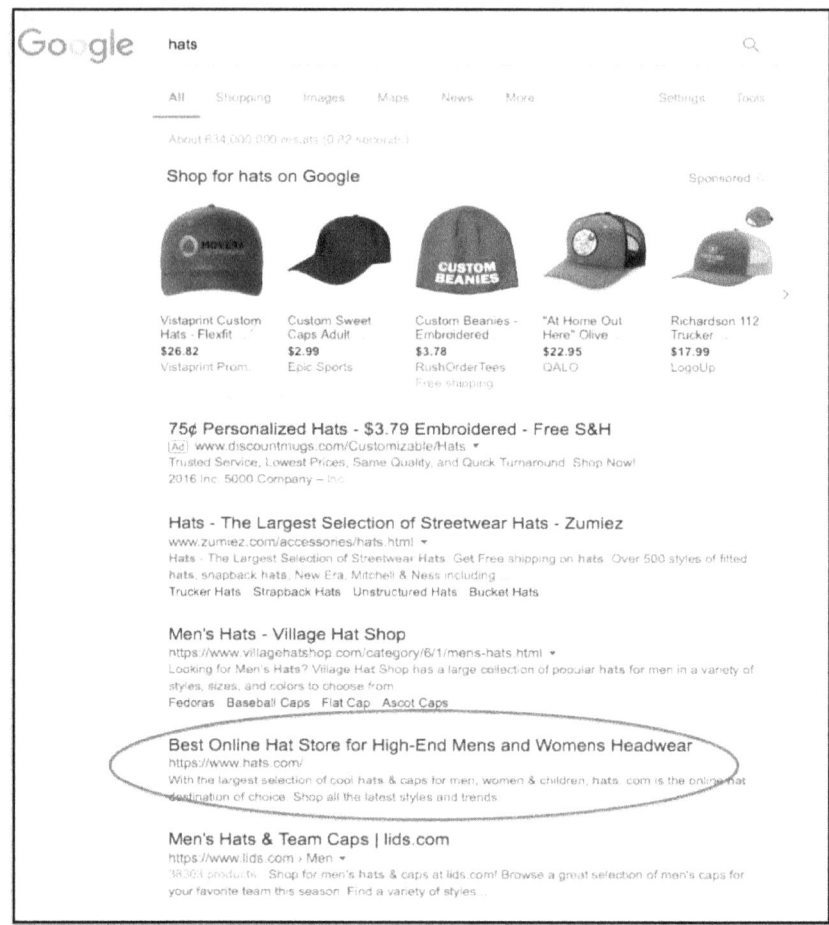

So, resist the urge to adopt sexy brand names for your business, products, or services. They will end up being your "page rank boat anchor". Instead, focus on names that will help you gain customer recognition, and save your marketing dollars for driving sales.

When choosing a name, the best place to start is by defining your target market and defining the benefits you will provide. A name that fits within these criteria then represents your value proposition.

> ***Restart Insight:*** *When developing your small business brand name or the name of your product or service names, avoid the temptation to create a sexy name that does not communicate a clear message to your customer about what you do, especially since that name can simultaneously hurt your page rank.*

Brand Name Creation in Action

As mentioned earlier, we will use a fictional company as an example as we move through the process of creating a brand. I have intentionally created a service that is easy to understand and won't distract you from the process of creating your brand name.

This small business is focused on helping provide software to nursing home providers of support for senior citizens.

Customer Segments	Benefits Provided
Nursing home facilities	**Time Savings, Convenience,**
	Cost Savings
Physicians	**Convenience, Time Savings**

Now we have identified the customer segments and benefits for each customer segment. In this case, "convenience" is a universal benefit. There might be a benefit to the primary customer, in this case, homebound seniors, that overrides all of the other benefits (e.g. safety of the homebound senior person).

A sound strategy is to combine your customer segment(s) with the benefit(s). This is a great time to use a website such as thesaurus.com to search for synonyms.

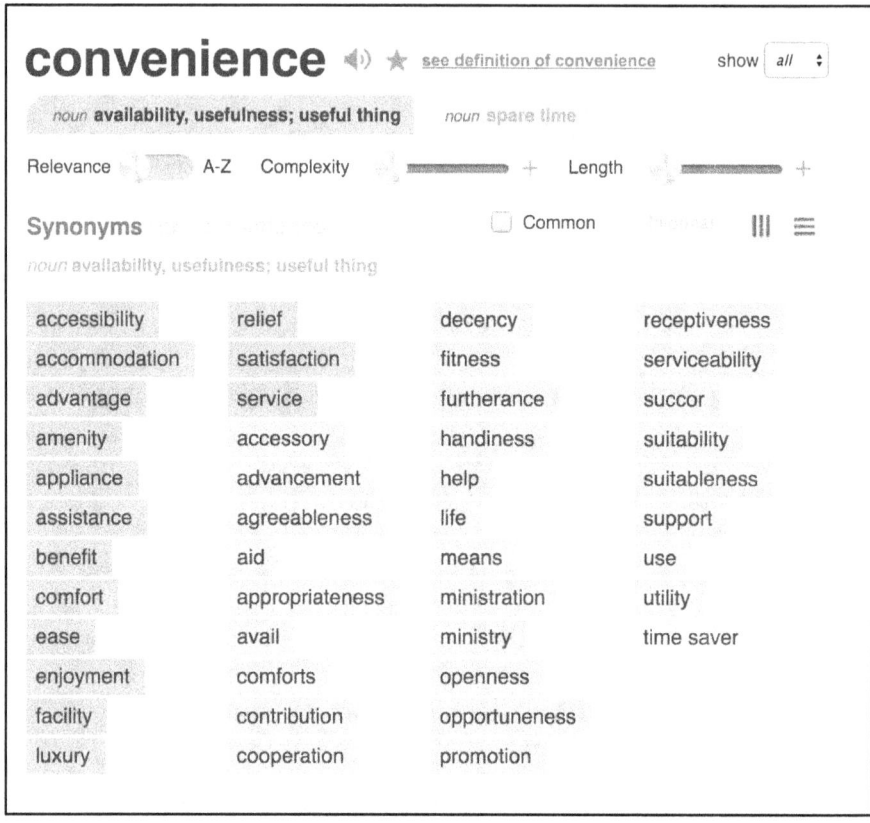

To continue with the example, let's select the word "senior" to represent our customer segment. Next, we decide that "convenience" is too vague, so we select "aid" instead.

In this case, let's create the brand name "Senior Aid."

1. Trademark Implications

Before moving on with selecting your brand name, you should search the United States Patent and Trademark Office website to ensure your brand name is not taken, so you can avoid trademark infringement. Simply go to uspto.gov. Consult your attorney for additional insights into using a trademark name if someone is already using the one you've chosen. You might find another company is using the name, but for a different product with a different target market. This could have very different implications than if a company is using the same name and targeting the same or similar customers.

You do not have to pay to register your trademark, but it is safest to do so. Trademarking the name gives you the most legal protection. Once you receive the trademark approval, begin putting the ® next to your brand name. However, many small businesses will simply put the "TM" next to their name if they are selling a product and "SM" if they selling a service. Using ™ or ℠ is basically a way of saying, "if you use our brand, we will file a complaint with the USPTO for using our brand name." However, in order to file a complaint, that company name must first be registered. As of the writing of this book, the cost to file for a trademark with the USPTO is $275. Obviously, you can pay your attorney to do it for you if you so choose.

There are more details to follow on trademarks in "Step 3 – Legally Protecting Your Small Business."

2. Selecting your Website Address

Your website address, also known as a URL (universal resource locator), is critically important to small businesses. It is one of the most efficient and effective ways to market your business, answer customer questions, and make sales.

You need to take a scientific approach to select your website address, because it will determine the amount of traffic you attract to your website, landing page, social media sites, etc. I see many small businesses just selecting something sexy that has no clear expression of what the company does. Sometimes they will select a website address that doesn't even match the brand name they have created. If you have $5 million to promote your brand, then ignore this section. If you don't, pay attention—the website address class is now in session.

First, check the availability on a website address service provider such as GoDaddy. There are less expensive services than them, but GoDaddy provides website addresses, website builder software, integrated payment services, hosting, email addresses, and more.

Returning to our fictional company, Senior Aid, we want to select a name for our website that is the same as our brand name. We will also need to consider the domain extension (e.g. .com, .net, .org). In general, it's best to check for a .com domain first. It is the most commonly used domain extension for businesses.

So, let's go to GoDaddy and type "senioraid.com" in the domain search field. You can see the results below.

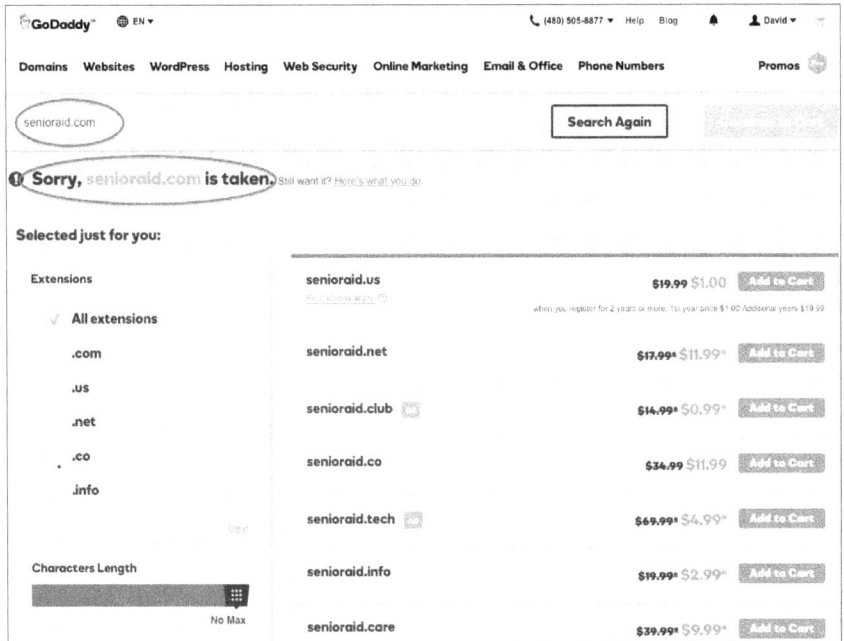

Unfortunately, in this case, senioraid.com is taken. Determining that someone has already purchased a website address that matches our brand can be a very deflating experience for small businesses.

However, all is not lost!

At this point we have three primary options:

1. Change the name of the website address we want to use (and also change our brand name).
2. Locate the owner of the website address and try to purchase it from them.
3. Select a website address with a different domain extension.

If you have spent a great deal of time creating your brand and have received positive feedback from prospective customers, stick with what you have and proceed to one of the last two options.

Check to see if there is an active website tied to the website address that we want to use. I typed "senioraid.com" into the address bar of the browser and this **blank page** popped up. The good news is the website address is probably not being used. The bad news is that we don't know who to contact to purchase the website address.

And here's more good news. There are web-based tools whereby you can locate the owner of a domain name. Let the detective work begin. I simply went to "ICANN Who Is" and typed in senioraid.com into the Lookup text box.

This is what popped up:

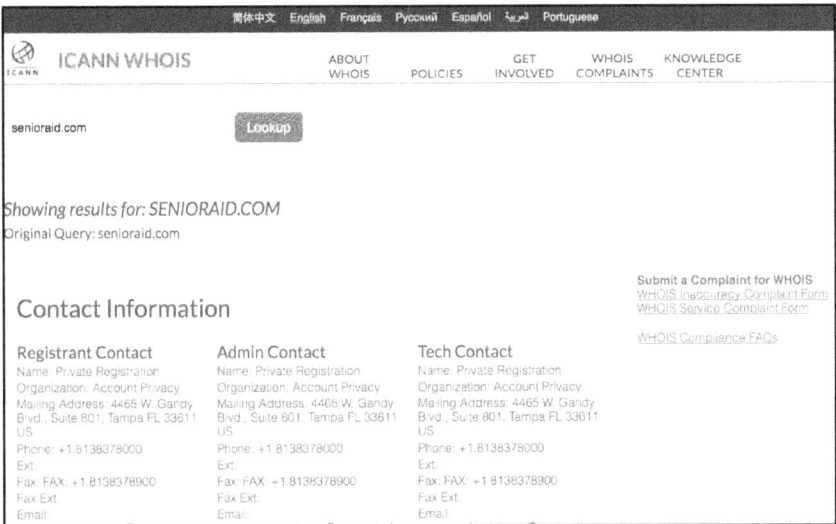

We have discovered there is a private owner of the website address. You will notice there is a phone number. Frequently, there is an email address and phone number of the "Registrant Contact," but unfortunately, in this case, we just have a phone number. So, I made the call to the phone number listed and got no answer. I can choose to keep calling or select another domain extension.

I do need to give you a heads-up on something that creates a great deal of pain for those legitimately seeking website addresses for their businesses. There are companies around the world that aggregate website addresses and resell them; they are sometimes known as domain squatters. We won't get into a discussion about how I feel about these companies, but given that one of my greatest passions is helping budding small businesses, you can probably imagine. These companies purchase URLs they think will be popular in the future and then turnaround and sell these website addresses, frequently for prices that first-time small businesses can't afford.

I had a friend that launched a tech small business (with which you are all familiar) in San Francisco, that experienced explosive growth. Unfortunately, I cannot share their name. They were absolutely set on their brand name, as were their investors who had invested tens of millions of dollars into the company. The website address holder found out who the small business was, and the good old rule of supply and demand kicked in. The squatter would not release the website address for less than $50k. His small business actually paid the $50k. Before you start feeling sorry for him, you should know that he ended up selling his company for $170 million.

I am not advocating you pay exorbitant prices for website addresses, especially when you are in efficiency mode and every dollar is precious. In fact, I recommend quite the opposite. Here is a strategy to deal with situations when you cannot locate a potential seller of a website address or when they are asking an astronomical price that just isn't practical for your small business.

Use another domain type such as .us, .net (which represents Internet service providers), or .org (which represents nonprofits).

Note: When we say nonprofits, we are not referring to small businesses that don't make a profit but, rather, organizations that are specifically not-for-profit such as charities.

One strategy used by startups and small businesses now, based on the number of .com website addresses that have been taken, is utilizing .io. The origin of .io is that it represents the "Indian Ocean." However, many tech firms will just say it represents "Input-Output."

Back to our Senior Aid example...

So, we search for senioraid.io. Voila! Senioraid.io is available. Next, we simply pay for the website address. We can also add an email connected to the website address. For example, if your name is Bob, you might select bob@senioraid.io.

Social Media Addresses

The next thing we want to do is check social media website address availability. There are services such as "KnowEm" that allow you to easily check the availability of all the major social media service providers. With the Senior Aid example YouTube and Facebook were available, but many others were unavailable.

I do not recommend eliminating a good brand name just because it lacks availability on social media. You can choose variations on the name or something descriptive as a way to secure a social media presence. The only time it's important to have your exact brand name in your social media presence is if you've found that your target market is going to primarily locate you through a specific social media platform or service. In this case, you may want to find a name that's more widely available on the platforms where your customers will be looking for you.

Creating Your Logo

Once we have created our brand name, purchased our website address, and checked the availability of social media addresses, we can move on to creating our logo. This part can be really fun (no sarcasm intended).

This is not one of those times to rely on your nephew who is a graphic designer taking a "gap year" to work as a ski lift operator in Vail™. There are many more rapid ways to get logo designs created. I recommend sources such as Fiverr fiverr.com or Elance elance.com. It is important to provide as much "creative direction" as possible when asking for a design.

Provide samples of other logos that you like. Provide the colors you desire. Interestingly, colors used on websites follow trends. I recommend conducting a search for the most popular colors if you are launching a business-to-consumer brand.

Choosing the Colors for your Brand

It is easy to just tell a graphic designer something like, "I like red and black—let's just go with that." However, we should consider the impact on consumer behavior.

There are considerations of emotion that are created by colors, which should be considered when creating your logo.

Some of the recurring themes are:

- Yellow connotes optimism.
- Orange connotes friendliness.
- Blue connotes trust and dependability.
- Red connotes excitement and power.
- Purple connotes creativity.
- Green connotes peacefulness.
- Gray connotes balance.

Providing Creative Direction

Some small businesses find the process of deciding on a logo laborious and frustrating. They complain about how the graphic designer is "not creative," "they don't understand," "they are not getting it," etc. Typically, these problems result from not providing the graphic designer enough "creative direction." Creative direction, in this context, refers to providing the graphic designer with clear, concise guidance.

Working with a graphic designer is a partnership. You'll want to tell them what your expectations are and provide some "must- haves" for the logo. For example, you might request that a graphic designer use the colors blue and white, the Arial font, and an image that represents teamwork. You may even know the exact color of blue you want to see. A good, seasoned graphic designer will welcome this guidance because it ensures that they'll deliver something that meets those needs in the first round. The closer you can get to "right" on the first round, the fewer rounds of changes you'll need to make and the less the work will cost. If a graphic designer gets defensive about simple direction, find a new graphic designer.

Providing some direction, while leaving room for the designer to apply their talent is critical. Remember, you're hiring them because they have the skills to do the work. Unless you're a trained artist or designer yourself, give them some latitude so they can deliver their best work. If your direction is too specific (Example: "I want a circle logo with a line through the center and I've sketched out how the name should look"), you're doing yourself a disservice. You'll end up with something YOU thought would be cool but might not have the necessary elements of a good, usable logo.

Finally, do not get hung up on the logo being perfect. If you get something that's good and representative of your business or product, use it for your pilot or your launch. You can always evolve it later on.

Marketing Your Small Business

Marketing 101

Here is a crash course in marketing if you are a non-marketer. **One of the mistakes non-marketers often make is equating "marketing" with "advertising" only**. Marketing is much more than advertising, and understanding this is critical for the small business owner.

There are four, core elements to marketing – commonly known as the 4Ps or your marketing mix.

1. Product
2. Place
3. Price
4. Promotion

Seasoned marketers will also add:

5. Process
6. People
7. Physical evidence
8. Performance

However, to keep things simple, we are going to focus on the classic "4Ps"

Marketing Mix (4Ps)

Marketing Plan Preparation

One of the temptations first-time small business owners face is diving right into the fun stuff—the marketing of their small business—before they have even created a validated business model. Resist the urge to think about marketing until you have validated your business model and have selected your brand name. Your completed business model is going to drive many of your marketing decisions.

If you are reading this step and have not achieved validation, please go back and validate your concept. I have seen too many small business owners throw all of their energy into the marketing of an idea when they should have spent it on business model discovery. Many of those have resulted in spectacular PUBLIC failures. Needless to say, this is not only bad for the small business itself, but it also damages the credibility of the small business owner.

If you have done your due diligence, have conducted discovery, prepared your family, created your Business Model Canvas, and developed your brand, it is now time to move on to creating your marketing plan.

In this section, we are going to create a very basic small business marketing plan. This plan can be expanded and refined if necessary but it will give you a place to start.

The critical elements of your marketing plan include:

1. Define your target market(s).
2. Create your value proposition.
3. Develop your pricing.
4. Build your sales channels.
5. Identify your distribution channels.
6. Create your advertising.
7. Develop your marketing calendar.

Note: Many marketing plans also include a comprehensive competitive analysis, which we did not create for our example business, Senior Aid.

Let's revisit Senior Aid and create a sample marketing plan.

Senior Aid Marketing Plan - Example

Customer Value Proposition

Senior Aid provides a software solution to help manage and communicate services provided to seniors who receive long-term care, in order to increase safety and convenience and provide peace of mind.

Customer segments:	Benefits provided:
Nursing homes	Safety, Time Savings, Convenience, Cost Savings
Children of nursing home seniors	Peace-of-mind, Convenience, Cost Savings
Nursing home team members	Convenience, Time Savings
Physicians & Nurses	Convenience, Time Savings

Priority Markets

We'll base Senior Aid's market priorities on market opportunity combined with market need, in this order:

1. Homebound seniors
2. Visiting nurses (organizations)
3. Physicians (clinics, hospitals, groups)

Services

Senior Aid will offer the following:

1. Web-based software application
2. Administrative portal for the senior long-term care management company
3. Individual health service provider portal
4. Family web portal (log-in)

5. Mobile application
6. Family portal
7. Family support provider referral program
8. Family support provider application
9. Family support provider selection process
10. Family support provider payment system to Senior Aid
11. Integrated payment system

Website

Because Senior Aid is a digital product, their website will be the hub of the sales channels' efforts. This will include access for healthcare service providers, families, and physicians. We need to invest time and financial resources into robust search engine optimization. At launch, we will also activate a paid search campaign on Google AdWords to drive initial traffic. Lastly, we will secure a banner ad on the AARP website (and link it to an AARP-specific landing page on our website). It's very important to also rapidly secure testimonial videos from family members and seniors and highlight those quotes on our website's home page.

Senior Aid Website Hub graphic:

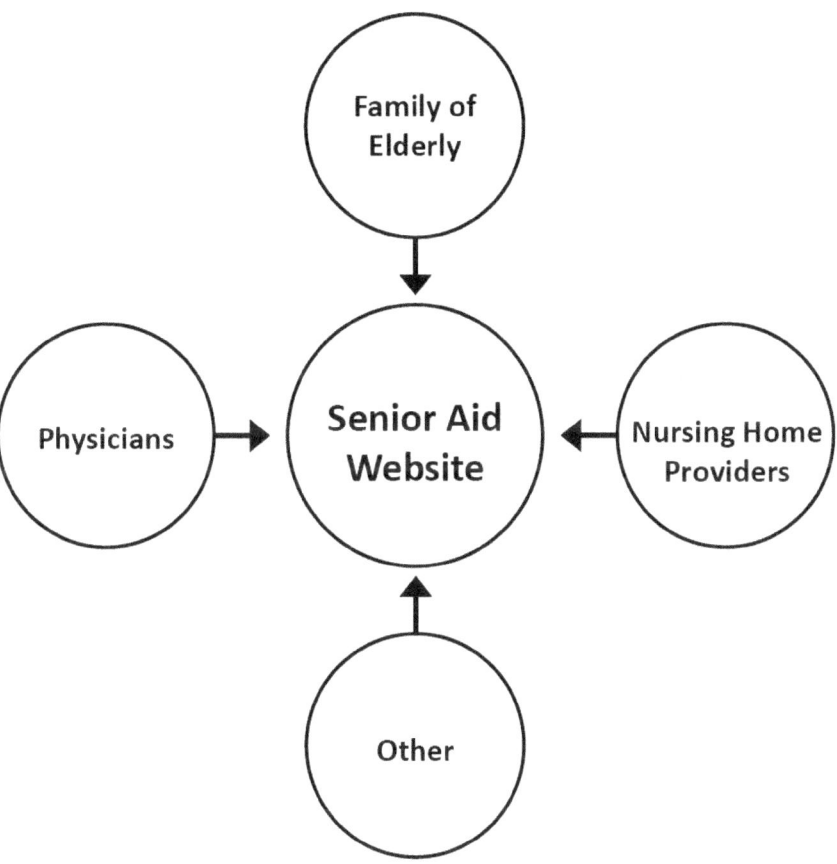

Logo

The Senior Aid logo will utilize blue and white in an effort to represent honesty and integrity. The shapes within the logo represent the unification of the family, the service provider, and the seniors through the support provided by Senior Aid. A square version of the logo will also be created so it can be effectively incorporated into social media.

Marketing Message

Senior Aid has various audiences with different needs. It is critical that all audiences are considered in marketing efforts. Below are the primary audiences, their needs, and the related messages we need to convey.

	Safety	Peace-of-Mind	Convenience	Time Savings	Profitability
Family	X	X	X		
Physicians			X	X	
Service Providers			X	X	X

You cannot use the same message or story for each audience. What the family needs to hear is very different from what the physicians and service providers need to hear. So, marketing campaigns need to focus the messages relative to each audience.

Family marketing messaging: Marketing campaigns targeting the families of the seniors receiving long-term care should focus on safety, peace-of-mind, and convenience.

Physicians marketing messaging: Marketing campaigns that target physicians should focus on convenience and time savings.

Service provider marketing messaging: Marketing campaigns targeting service providers should deliver a message that focuses on convenience, time savings, and profitability.

Senior Aid Pricing

Our initial pricing model is below. Senior Aid will focus on the Basic and Plus plans during their pilot phase.

	Basic	Plus	Pro
Senior Aid Platform	Yes	Yes	Yes
Mobile App	Yes	Yes	Yes
Nursing Home Portal	Yes	Yes	Yes
Family Portal	N/A	Yes	Yes
Private Training	N/A	N/A	Yes
Custom Dashboard	N/A	N/A	Yes
Phone Support	N/A	N/A	Yes
Monthly Price	$199	$399	$599

Promotion

Most first-time small businesses jump straight to the "promotion" element of the 4Ps and focus on advertising without considering pricing. The following methodology shows how you can prioritize the market based on impact.

Each of these marketing methodologies is listed in chronological order based on priority. The priority is based on efficiency and effectiveness. This means you should use methods that deliver the highest sales impact first – often referred to as the "low hanging fruit", meaning the easiest customers to sell. For our example, this includes methods that get the newest service provider sign-ups for the lowest cost and shortest time commitment. With additional financial resources (e.g. from revenue and external investment) and additional labor (e.g. hiring of business development managers and marketers), we can become more aggressive.

Target-market Matrix with the Applicable Marketing Methods:

	Senior Aid Website	Business Development (Emails, webinars, sales calls)	Paid Search Advertising	Trade shows	Public Relations and Social Media
Nursing Homes	1	2	5	4	3
Families	1	N/A	2	N/A	3
Physicians	1	5	N/A	N/A	2

Business Development (Sales) Efforts

"Sales" is in the job description of every single person in a small business. If you haven't communicated that to all your team members, it is time to do so. Whether you have a retail shop, restaurant, insurance company, car dealership, bank, construction, professional services company, or any other small business it is everyone's job to sell! Unfortunately, many small businesses wait until a crisis happens to set this expectation. If you haven't done it yet do it now.

What is this Selling Thing of Which You Speak?

Obviously, all companies began as startups, which is sometimes easy to forget. At the beginning of every company's life, the focus needs to be on refining the business model with a laser focus on customer acquisition (sales growth). Without that focus on sales, small businesses either die or bounce along the road without ever truly thriving. During this phase, business development/salespeople need to give customers the white glove treatment. White-glove treatment leads to increased revenue and referrals, and the cycle continues.

However, as these startups grow into sustainable small businesses, processes are tightened to increase efficiencies, employees develop specializations, products are refined, and services are delivered in fewer steps. Typically, disconnects begin to appear between customers and the company.

These disconnects also cause employees to be further and further removed from the customers—their needs, problems with products and services, ideas for product improvements, etc. As a result, in many organizations, large swaths of employees are completely out of touch with customers. They also either lose or never had, a focus on sales.

"Sales" is in the job description of every single person in a small business If you are an army of one, your primary goal is to continue to grow the business. If you have engineers, they need to focus on product development. Your engineers need to be responsive to urgent needs to change the user experience. If you have finance people, they need to keep a very close eye on your cash flow. But if the entire team isn't committed to growing the company through sales, ultimately the startup will never take off.

Interview: Kathy Hust, Kathy Hust Enterprises

Kathy Hust, is an angel investor, mentor for the gener8tor startup accelerator and consultants to startups, small businesses as well as high growth businesses, and is the CEO for Kathy Hust Enterprises. Kathy also sits on two corporate boards and she is a former regional vice president for U.S. Cellular. Kathy and I have known each other for over 25 years and her ability to rapidly grow a business through strong leadership is absolutely mind-boggling. She was the perfect person to interview about how important a commitment to sales is, regardless of the size of the business.

While at U.S. Cellular, Kathy led a sales and operations team of 2,800 sales and operations people that consistently delivered double-digit, year-over-year growth. She also was the president of a rapidly growing early-stage company, Scanalytics. She also mentors startups and small businesses on a regular basis. Kathy discussed with me her concern regarding the lack of focus on sales at small companies.

"Sometimes when I am mentoring startup and small businesses, I am shocked at the lack of recognition of the importance of sales. At times, some team members might focus too much on product development; meanwhile, they are burning through cash and not growing the business. At one small business, the founders and I had regular meetings where we discussed the primary activities from the previous week.

At each meeting, I asked for an update on sales results. During one particular meeting one of the founders stated, "Well, we had a call last week from X company (a Fortune 500 company) that wanted to buy our product." I responded, "That is fantastic, where are we at with them? What are the next steps?" The response I received from one of the founders shocked me. "Well, we told them that we were too busy working with a supplier and didn't have the time to meet with them." Needless to say, we had a very direct conversation about how critical sales were to their business and that if they continued down this same path, they were simply not going to survive. ***All businesses, need to have all employees focus on generating*** *sales all the time. This need is even more heightened during times of chaos."*

Restart Insight: *Sales is the ultimate priority in a small business and is in EVERYONE's job description.*

An easy incentive to get everyone on your team focused on sales is to provide commissions or company bonuses to all employees based on the new business they generate. Who is to say that you couldn't pay your bookkeeper, your customer service people, your technician, your waitstaff, or your receptionist a commission? Just make sure you set clear expectations on what qualifies as a new business, who will get paid, when they will get paid and how they will get paid. If you don't these initiatives can create more anger than sales productivity.

If individual commissions or bonuses don't work for you, implement team-based or company incentives based on new customers, new revenue, etc. For example, if the company reaches a particular sales-based goal, you'll treat the entire team to a pizza party or a happy hour at a favorite local spot. These incentives should be something that everyone enjoys and actually encourages them to work hard at always selling for your company.

So, get everyone focused on growth!

3) Marketing Efforts: Inbound vs Outbound

When working to capture leads for the members of your sales team, there are two types of marketing tactics: inbound and outbound. The goal of these tactics is simple, attract people who are otherwise unfamiliar with your offering, nurture them until they set up a demo or make a purchase, and finally, provide support after the purchase. In the case of Senior Aid, we need to drive traffic to our website to register for demos, so we'll focus on the tactics below.

Outbound:

1) Paid Search Campaigns
   Internet paid search campaigns (e.g. Google AdWords) will assist in driving website traffic. This process involves using Google's Keyword Estimator Tool, ad creation, and launch. Each campaign can be geo-targeted. This means campaigns will appear in designated areas based on IP address.

2) Trade Shows
   For our example business, Senior Aid, trade shows will become a critical marketing component that we will use to reach medical service centers. We will need to identify the most efficient and effective conferences to drive the most sign-ups.

3) Social Media Ads
   We will use the targeting options on social media to narrow our reach to seniors and their families. We will use images and video content related to in-home senior care and will direct viewers to our website. We will then use custom audiences and retargeting ads to reach those who have visited our site until they set up a demo.

4) Public Relations (PR)
   Public relations will target large market media outlets and the American Association of Retired Persons (AARP). We will also reach out to local media outlets with the success stories of the seniors we serve.

5) Email Marketing
   We will use forms on our website to capture the email addresses of our visitors. We will set up automated email marketing campaigns to engage with our target audience on an ongoing basis.

We will start by providing resources such as "The ultimate guide to choosing the right level of care for your loved one," or "The top 10 things needed for the most comfortable care," and progressively ask for more involvement, such as an initial-needs call and ultimately a demo.

Inbound:

1) Social Media Organic Content

YouTube: Our social media efforts will be driven by videos and testimonials from families. We will have separate software demo videos for home health care providers.

Facebook: We will use Facebook as our customer engagement platform. It will be critical not only to provide customer experience videos and tips for caring for loved ones but also to monitor posts for potential customer problems

We will also publish short-form content on Facebook that covers the life stories of the seniors we serve and the caregivers who provide the servicing. This will help build an emotional connection with our audience and expand our reach.

2) Blog Posts

We will develop a series of blogs related to the most commonly asked questions about in-home senior care. To find these topics, we'll use a service like **Answer The Public** or **Google Trends**.

*****Important Note** When setting up the marketing plan for your small business, determine what your competitors are doing. Pay special attention to the channels they are present and the specific ways they are positioning their offering. Sign up for their email newsletter, their webinars, and their demos. Do not simply copy the actions they are taking; learn from them.

In the past, I've found that most leads come from one or two sources. Try to figure out where the gaps are (where your competitors aren't present) and focus on owning those channels. If your competitors have the most engagement on YouTube and webinars but don't have any paid search campaigns or content on Facebook, try developing paid search and Facebook first.

Lastly, you need to coordinate all of these activities. Whether you have a team of people or it's just you running the show, creating a marketing calendar is critical. Managing your marketing without a plan will lead to missed sales opportunities and could even be fatal to your small business.

So, take the time to create a marketing calendar. Even something very basic like this:

Marketing Calendar (1st quarter)

	Jan	Feb	Mar	Person Responsible	Notes:
Tradeshow				Tom	Research the most cost-effective trade shows.
Business Development			X	Mary & Bob	Hire Mary & Bob full-time by Mar 1.
Paid Search Advertising	X	X	X	Eli	Set up a monthly budget by Dec 15.
Social Media		X	X	Sam and Anna	Provide 2 posts per week on Facebook and Twitter. Upload campaign videos to Facebook. Respond to new follows and messages.
Channel Partnerships			X	Kristen, Bob	Launch pilots on recommended channels from AARP.
Associations			X	Dave	Join 1-2 associations to gather contacts and begin business development efforts.

Step 3 – Legally Protecting Your Small Business

NOTE: Startup Guides, LLC, and the author provide information only and do not provide legal advice. Please consult an attorney before making any legal decisions for your business.

There are five primary areas of legal consideration for the small business.

1. Structure of the entity
2. Contracts
3. Compliance and licensing
4. Intellectual property (IP)
5. Funding

Some small businesses don't create legal structures for their businesses which exposes the owners to personal liability when customers or others take legal action. The loss of personal assets simply isn't worth the risk.

Secondly, some small businesses need to change legal structure. For example, you might have started your business as an LLC* and then take an investment from outside investors which might necessitate you changing the legal structure to a C-Corp.** See the definitions of LLCs and C Corps in the next section "Legal Structure Options."

Legal Structure Options

Sole Proprietorship

A sole proprietorship is easy to form and gives you complete control of your business. You're automatically considered to be a sole proprietorship if you do business activities but don't register as any other kind of business. Sole proprietorships do not produce a separate business entity. This means your business assets and liabilities are not separate from your personal assets and liabilities. You can be held personally liable for the debts and obligations of the business. Sole proprietors are still able to get a company name, even though it isn't a legal entity. It can be hard to raise money since you can't sell the stock, and banks are hesitant to lend to sole proprietorships. Sole proprietorships can be a good choice for low-risk businesses and owners who want to test their business idea before forming a more formal business.

Partnership

A partnership is the simplest structure for two or more people to own a business together. There are two common kinds of partnerships: limited partnerships (LP) and limited liability partnerships (LLP). Limited partnerships have only one general partner with unlimited liability, and all other partners have limited liability. The partners with limited liability also tend to have limited control over the company, which is documented in a partnership agreement. Profits are passed through to personal tax returns, and the general partner—the partner without limited liability—must also pay self-employment taxes. Limited liability partnerships are similar to limited partnerships, but give limited liability to every owner. An LLP protects each partner from debts against the partnership, and they won't be responsible for the actions of other partners. Partnerships can be a good choice for businesses with multiple owners, professional groups (like attorneys), and groups who want to test their business idea before forming a more formal business.

Limited Liability Company (LLC)*

An LLC lets you take advantage of the benefits of both the corporation and partnership business structures. LLCs protect you from personal liability in most instances. This means your personal assets, like your vehicle, house, and savings accounts, won't be at risk in case your LLC faces bankruptcy or lawsuits.

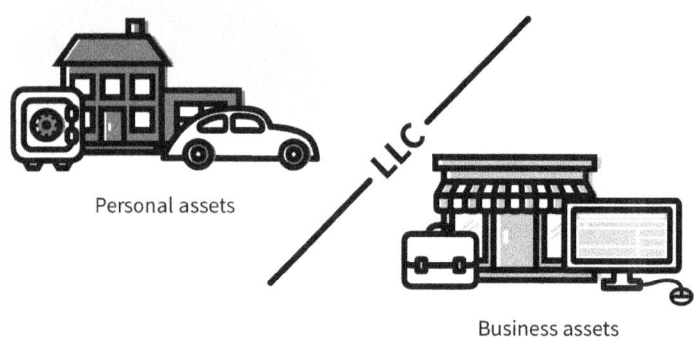

Profits and losses can get passed through to your personal income without facing corporate taxes. However, members of an LLC are considered self-employed and must pay self-employment tax contributions toward Medicare, and Social Security. LLCs can have a limited life in many states. When a member joins or leaves an LLC, some states may require the LLC to be dissolved and re-formed with new membership—unless there's already an agreement in place within the LLC for buying, selling, and transferring ownership. LLCs can be a good choice for medium- or higher-risk businesses, owners with significant personal assets they want to be protected, and owners who want to pay a lower tax rate than they would pay with a corporation.

Corporations

C Corp**

A C corporation (or C Corp) is a legal entity that is separate from its owners. Corporations can make a profit, be taxed be held legally liable. A corporation offers the strongest protection to its owners from personal liability, but the cost to form a corporation is higher than other structures. Corporations also require more extensive record-keeping, operational processes, and reporting. Unlike sole proprietors, partnerships, and LLCs, corporations pay income tax on their profits. In some cases, corporate profits are taxed twice—first, when the company makes a profit, and again when dividends are paid to shareholders on their personal tax returns.
Corporations have completely independent lives separate from their shareholders. If a shareholder leaves the company or sells his or her shares, the C corp can continue doing business relatively undisturbed. Corporations have an advantage when it comes to raising capital because they can raise funds through the sale of stock, which can also be a benefit in attracting employees. Corporations can be a good choice for medium- or higher-risk businesses, businesses that need to raise money, and businesses that plan to "go public" or eventually be sold.

S Corp

An S corporation (or S Corp) is a special type of corporation that's designed to avoid the double taxation drawback of a regular C corp. An S corp allows profits, and some losses, to be passed through directly to the owner's personal income without ever being subject to corporate tax rates. Not all states tax S corps equally, but most recognize them the same way the federal government does, therefore taxing the shareholders accordingly. Some states tax S corps on profits above a specified limit, while others don't recognize the S corp election at all; they simply treat the business as a C corp.

S corps must file with the IRS to get S Corp status, which is a different process than registering with their state. There are special limits on S corps. S corps can't have more than 100 shareholders, and all shareholders must be U.S. citizens. You will still have to follow the strict filing and operational processes of a C corp. S corps also have an independent life, just like C corps. If a shareholder leaves the company or sells his or her shares, the S corp can continue doing business relatively undisturbed. S corps can be a good choice for businesses that would otherwise be a C corp, but meet the criteria to file as an S corp.

B Corp

A benefit corporation (or B corp) is a for-profit corporation recognized in a majority of U.S. states. B corps are different from C corps in purpose, accountability, and transparency, but aren't different in how they're taxed. B corps are driven by both mission and profit. Shareholders hold the company accountable to produce some sort of public benefit in addition to a financial profit. Some states require B corps to submit annual benefit reports that demonstrate their contributions to the public good. There are several third-party B corp certification services, but none are required for a company to be legally considered a B corp in those states where the legal status is available.

Close Corporation

Close corporations resemble B corps but have a less traditional corporate structure. These shed many formalities that typically govern corporations and those that apply to smaller companies. State rules vary, but shares are usually barred from public trading. Close corporations can be run by a small group of shareholders without a board of directors.

Nonprofit Corporation

Nonprofit corporations are organized to do charitable, educational, religious, literary, or scientific work. Because their work benefits the public, nonprofits can receive tax-exempt status, meaning they don't pay state or federal income taxes on any profits they make.

Nonprofits must file with the IRS to get tax exemption, which again is a different process from registering with their state. Nonprofit corporations need to follow organizational rules very similar to a regular C corp. They also need to follow special rules about what they do with any profits they earn. For example, they can't distribute profits to members or political campaigns. Nonprofits are often called 501(c)(3) corporations—a reference to the section of the Internal Revenue Code that is most commonly used to grant tax-exempt status.

Source: Small Business Administration, 10/7/2017

Example: Registering for an LLC:

I cannot provide legal advice as to which legal entity type you should select. However, I needed to set up a legal entity for a new company of mine, **Startup Guides**, so I thought I would share the process I followed. Startup Guides provides small business training programs and mentoring, and it will serve as the publishing company for this and future books.

The ease and cost of filing for legal entity status do vary by state. Wisconsin, where Startup Guides is headquartered, happens to make this process very simple, affordable, and fast. I completed the forms on the Wisconsin Department of Financial Institutions website in 10 minutes, paid $130, and my filing went off for approval. I received approval with the official designation of the legal entity status of Startup Guides LLC within five business days. Below is the initial screen of the process to file for Startup Guides LLC. You will notice at the beginning of this book that this material is copyrighted and owned by that business with the designation © 2020- Startup Guides LLC.

Note: Some states will charge closer to $1,000 and may take up to two months to process. So, if you are in need of creating immediate legal status for your company (like when you have an urgent contract), plan accordingly.

Contracts

Contracts can be very intimidating to the first-time small business owner. There are non-competes, non-disclosure agreements, operating agreements, license agreements, independent contractor agreements, project financing agreements, and more.

The term "agreements" is often used instead of "contracts." This is softer and less intimidating language and generally more widely used. Going forward in the book, we will be using the term agreements, not contracts. Just remember, "agreements" are "contracts" and will have the same, legally-binding importance.

There are four categories of agreements:

1. Commercial
2. Human resources
3. Transactional
4. Intellectual property (IP)

Here are examples within each category:

Commercial

a. Vendor
b. Customer
c. Franchise
d. Marketing
e. Outsourcing
f. Supply
g. Procurement
h. Operations

Human Resources

    a. Founders
    b. Employee
    c. Consultancy
    d. Non-compete
    e. Non-solicitation
    f. Stock options

Transactional

    a. Joint Venture
    b. Merger and Acquisition
    c. Investments
    d. Shareholder
    e. Concession
    f. Project Financing

Intellectual Property

    a. Non-disclosure
    b. License
    c. Assignment
    d. Technology Transfer
    e. Data Protection

Let's take a look at some of the agreements that are generally most important for small businesses.

Customer Agreements - Written agreements between a buyer and a seller. First-time small businesses frequently fall into the trap of doing business on a handshake when they are desperate for new business. This makes them appear unprofessional and unprepared and has many other negative ramifications (e.g. nonpayment).

Founders' Agreements - Written agreements that govern the relationship between the founders. These agreements are critical. It is extremely rare when founders decide to leave their company at the same time. People quit, get fired, get divorced, die, etc. Not planning for these scenarios is a bad idea. It is critical that the founders put an agreement in place as soon as they begin their business relationship.

Independent Contractor Agreements - Written agreements between a company and an independent contractor. Many small businesses also do business with a handshake when it comes to independent contractors. There are many bad reasons for not getting a contractor agreement in place. One of the primary reasons is clarifying the point that they are employed as "work for hire" and that your small business owns the work that the independent contractors create (in return for payment). Non-disclosure agreements and non-solicitation provisions should be included within independent contractor agreements.

Remember from our previous section on hiring, you need to be extremely careful not to classify people as contractors when they should be classified as employees.

Investor Agreements - Agreements between investors and current business owners that describe the terms of the investment, in addition to those for reporting and control.

Non-Disclosure Agreements (NDA) - Written agreements that protect the intellectual property of the owner. There are two types:

1. **Unilateral NDA** - Agreement whereby one party agrees not to reveal information to another party.

2. **Mutual NDA** - Agreement whereby both parties agree not to reveal information to another party.

Non-Compete Agreements - Agreement where an employee or other party (such as an independent contractor) agrees not to work for, or start, a similar company over a specified amount of time and within a geographical area.

Intellectual Property

There are four categories of Intellectual Property (IP) that every small business owner needs to understand:
1. Trademarks
2. Copyrights
3. Patents
4. Industrial Designs

1) Trademarks - A word, brand name, or symbol to indicate the owner. There are two types of trademarks: registered trademarks and unregistered trademarks. Trademarks for unregistered **products** utilize the ™ designation. The ™ stands for "trademark." Trademarks for unregistered **services** utilize the ℠ designation. The ℠ stands for "service mark."

Product Example: If you wanted to denote a trademark for a brand of sunglasses, a product, you would use ™ after your brand name.

Service Example: If you wanted to denote a trademark for software as a service (SaaS), you would utilize ℠ it after your brand name.

Although federal registration of a mark is not mandatory, it has several advantages, including notice to the public of the registrant's claim of ownership of the mark, a legal presumption of ownership nationwide, and exclusive right to use the mark on or in connection with the goods/services listed in the registration. You do need federal registration in order to file a lawsuit against someone you accuse of infringement.

Once trademarks are registered with the United States Patent and Trademark Office, both products and services use the ® designation. Registration is mandatory for protection.

2) Copyrights - Rights granted to the creator of literary, dramatic, musical, artistic, or other intellectual works. Registration is not mandatory for protection.

Copyright of this book example: You will notice near the beginning of this book, it states the copyright ©2020 - Startup Guides, LLC. This provides notification that the content of this book cannot be reproduced without the permission of my Small Business training and publishing company, Startup Guides LLC. As a side note, you have probably noticed already, I am here to help small businesses, so I will most likely be very accommodating if you do decide to reproduce a portion of the book, as long as you get written permission from my company first.

3) Patents - Right granted for an invention that provides a new, unique product or process. To receive patent protection, registration is mandatory.

Patent example: The Apple Ring patent outlines plans to develop a smart, interactive ring that syncs with other Apple devices such as the iPhone or iPad, and can alert the wearer when a text, tweet or status update is received. In the place of a traditional jewel or stone, there is a touchpad touchscreen and the ring could also include a microphone for picking up voice commands.

4) Industrial Designs - New product or packaging design in the form of a shape, configuration, pattern, or composition that is either two-dimensional (2D) or three-dimensional (3D). For protection, registration is mandatory.

Industrial design example: Coca Cola's contour bottle.

Tax Compliance

Your small business, whether incorporated or not, is subject to federal, state, and local tax compliance requirements from the time it is formed.

Relevant areas of tax compliance include:

a) Federal and state corporate income tax
b) Payroll taxes
c) Real and personal property taxes
d) Sales tax and the like

Be sure to obtain a federal employer identification number (EIN), so you are properly registered at the state and local level. It's also important to understand what filings and other compliance are required. Small Business-friendly tax accountants are typically the best places to provide this advice since they can address your ongoing tax return filing obligations as well as the initial registrations.

Investor Documentation

If you accept investments from friends and family or other third parties, you will need to document the terms of those investments and get advice about securities law. Convertible debt or simple agreements for future equity (SAFEs) are frequently used at the very early stages to minimize legal expenses and avoid the need for more detailed investor arrangements. However, the terms of these agreements, which create rights designed to convert into convertible preferred stock in the future, are beyond the scope of this book. See your attorney.

Employment

In addition to payment and withholding of payroll taxes, you will be subject to other mandatory requirements with respect to employees, including the procurement of workers' compensation and unemployment compensation insurance. Make sure you understand those obligations.

Insurance

Finally, you should get advice from an insurance broker as to the kinds of business insurance that are appropriate for a small business at your stage. The U.S. is a litigious country, and you need to consider what insurance you wish to carry even at the very earliest stage of your business.

Source: Gust, Bob Mollen - Fried, Frank, Harris, Shriver & Jacobson

Licensing

The Basic Concept of Licensing:

To license is simply to grant another person the right to use some asset one owns for a particular purpose and, usually, for a particular payment or series of payments termed a "royalty."

Most commonly, a party (business or individual) licenses the right to sell or exploit some assets that they own, such as intellectual property, a product, or a methodology. A few examples include a license to develop and promote a patented product and sell that same product in a particular territory; a license to use a particular product as part of a blend of products that are sold; a license to utilize a trade name or logo to sell a product in a particular locale; the license to publish a copyrighted work one has written, etc.

A license is usually reduced to a written contract specifying the rights, duties, and payments that are part of the license. A license can give all rights to exploit the asset to the licensee ("exclusive licensee") or only some of the rights to use in conjunction with other persons ("nonexclusive" or "limited" license.) The license normally grants full rights to the licensee to exploit as the licensee sees fit but may have certain performance criteria or a date when the license lapses or becomes nonexclusive.

Normally, the theme of a license is that the licensor is passive, merely receiving royalty payments, while the licensee engages in the business or development and is free to exploit so long as royalties are paid and other criteria are met. Failure to abide by the license agreement by the licensee normally results in termination of the license, as well as payment of damages to the licensor.

Unlike the sale of an asset, the licensor continues as the ultimate owner of the asset or methodology; limited rights to use what the licensor owns are transferred, but not ownership. The alternative to a license is the actual sale of the asset to the purchaser, but most licensors wish to continue as owners, so that they may exploit the asset in the future or other territories or applications. It is vital for the licensee to realize that unlike full ownership, a license is merely a group of rights that the licensee obtains with ownership of the whole remaining with the licensor.

Typical Licensing Issues to Confront:

Who Owns What? It is vital to define precisely what rights are being licensed, for how long and in what context. If the licensor owns the other assets or concepts that the licensor is exploiting on its own or transferring to third parties, it is important to make full disclosure so that the licensee does not claim that it is facing competition from licensor's other activities and that the license is valueless. Related to this are variations and improvements on the product or concept, discussed below.

How Long, What Price? What does the licensor get from the license? What payments are due when? Is there any guaranteed amount or just a percentage of sales? How are sales computed? How long does it last? What performance criteria must the licensee accomplish to maintain the license? How can the licensee abandon the license and move on to other products and can either the licensor or licensee compete with the product or method with their own or a third party's product or method?

Who Defends What? Particularly with trade names or intellectual property, it is important to define who has the duty to defend against third parties violating rights to the intellectual property, and that can be an expensive process. For example, if the licensor licenses a software design that a third-party claim was stolen, who must defend the claim and pay any damages? This should all be defined precisely in the agreement.

Improvements and Changes. Assuming that the licensor develops an improvement or the next generation of products, does the licensee have the right to exploit that improvement? This is vital to consider since the licensee may create a thriving business, only to discover that the licensor has licensed a new product that utterly undercuts the business created by the licensee. Further, if the licensee comes up with a variation or improvement, does that generate any rights in the licensor?

Role of Other Licensees. If the license is nonexclusive, what protections may exist to stop the other licensee from interfering with sales of the current licensee? How are disputes between the licensees resolved?

Right to Assign? Right to Co-Venture? Often the licensee will wish to bring in other entities to assist in its efforts to promote the product or service or will seek to sell its own license to another party. What rights does the licensor have to object or approve of such steps?

Right of Licensee to Alter the Product or Service. Typically, a licensee comes up with its own ideas or variations to the licensed product, either alone or in conjunction with third parties or when a customer requests a customized variation. What rights does the licensee have to alter the product or service?

Advertising and Promotional Materials. Often a licensor will want approval rights as to all marketing, training, and advertising materials. Usually, the licensee wants freedom of action and does not want the licensor, who may not be well versed in marketing or local conditions, to have veto power.

Indemnity Provisions. Most licensors want full protection, including insurance coverage, for the activities of the licensees. Most licensees want product liability carried by the licensor. The extent of such provisions is often an area of tense negotiations.

Local Regulations and Laws. Many locales, especially Europe, have extremely strict regulations as to products and services and restrictions on the right to trade and sell. Indeed, often local law can void contrary provisions in the license agreement. Some products considered safe and legal in a particular jurisdiction are illegal in others. A good example is alcohol sold in some Arab nations. It is vital to check applicable laws and regulations.

Taxes and Licenses. It is equally vital to allocate who is responsible for what taxes that may accrue. Normally, the licensee wants to not be involved in sales or employment activities and wants to be held harmless from all such liabilities. To achieve that, careful attention must be paid to the structure created in the agreement, since some jurisdictions may impose pseudo employment taxation in certain license arrangements. Of course, local business licenses must be paid and kept up to date by the licensee.

Standard Contract Issues. In addition to the numerous applicable issues that a particular project must consider, the standard terms and conditions and issues relating to them in any business contract must be considered.

Why License?

There are many ways businesses can join efforts to promote and sell a product or service, ranging from joint ownership of a single entity to joint ventures (partnerships of two or more entities) to distribution and sales representative arrangements. In most cases, a license is a method preferred by a person or entity who simply wants an entirely passive role. An example is receiving royalties, with no involvement in the day-to-day or even strategic marketing decisions. As one client put it, "I just want to sit back and cash my royalty checks."

But it is seldom that simple. The activities of the licensee must be of keen interest to any wise licensor since a bad or poorly performing licensee can result in a product or service that could have developed a good cash flow becoming useless, while other competing products come to dominate the field. Further, most licensees need guidance and assistance from the licensor, so inevitably more than "cashing the checks" is involved. While many inventors dream of licensing their product to some multinational that will simply pay a great deal of money over time, the average license involves two relatively small businesses that have to work together to make the process successful.

Licensing a product or service can be an excellent way to generate good cash flow if the document is properly created. This means there is a clear understanding of the goals and duties of both parties. More often than not, a license is limited in scope so that the licensor is free to develop certain markets or work with more than one licensee. It is vital to keep not only good legal advice in mind but to get good tax advice and local knowledge before commencing the relationship. If done well, an inventor or developer of a product or service can minimize his or her involvement in the work of marketing and delivering the service or product, while still receiving a good income.

Source: Stimmel, Stimmel & Smith P.C.

Step 4 – Raising Capital for Your Small Business

For small businesses that need more capital to thrive there are traditional options as well as new and creative options that small businesses might not have considered before.

There are a few primary options to raise capital for your small business:

1. Bootstrapping
2. Friends and Family
3. Banks and credit unions
4. Community development financial institutions
5. Crowdfunding
6. Online lenders
7. Angel investors & Venture capitalists
8. SBIR grants

Bootstrapping

Bootstrapping, as the name implies, is the act of self-funding a small business. Some consider only funds from the small business owner as true bootstrap funds. Others will include "Friends and Family" and others include crowdfunding.

Although bootstrapping can cause a small business to launch and grow at a slower pace than if it receives outside funding, the rich infusion of ready cash from investors can create a false sense of security, leading to poor decision-making. Think of that rich kid whose parents showered him/her with cash, never allowing their child to develop skills to become self-sufficient.

Bootstrapping forces small businesses to move rapidly to revenue generation. They also must carefully manage cash for operations and hire only high-impact team members. These all increase the probability of long-term success for the small business.

Some of the most common sources of personal funding include:

- Savings
- Home equity lines of credit
- Early retirement disbursements
- Credit cards

Taking early retirement disbursements is generally a last resort due to early withdrawal penalties and the loss of the compounding effect of your gains. Likewise, I don't advocate using high-interest credit cards. However, the reality is that low-interest credit cards are frequently used. In general, post-2008, banks are extremely risk-averse and tend not to provide loans to small business companies. The old adage of "banks only loan money to people who have it" frequently rings true. It is important to note that "community banks" tend to be more focused on the local economy and willing to work with small businesses than larger regional, national, and international banks. An excellent example of a community bank is First Citizens Bank. An interview with their CEO is in this chapter.

Having a conversation with your spouse/significant other about the maximum investment you are both willing to make and the sources of the funds is crucial. I know of a small business owner who took on $20,000 in credit card debt without talking with his spouse, and it wreaked havoc on their marriage.

I recommend having easy access to a minimum of twelve months of cash to cover your family's living expenses. However, this is not always realistic.

Friends and Family Money

The second most popular source of small business funding behind self-funding are friends and family.

According to statistics on the Fundable crowdfunding website, friends and family are a major funding source for all small businesses, investing over $60 billion in new ventures in 2016, almost triple the amount coming from venture capital sources. The average amount raised from venture capital sources per small business was $23k, usually in the form of a convertible loan, rather than an equity investment.

The benefits of using "Friends and Family" money include: rapid access to funds; money is frequently provided with no expectation of a return of the capital, nor any interest; and they most commonly do not require the small business owner to provide equity in return for the capital.

Be aware that sometimes family members providing funds feel they have a strong influence on how the business should be run, even though they lack the small business experience and knowledge to guide the business.

One of the most significant things that can occur, when a business accepts money from friends or family, is a negative impact on relationships in the event that the business folds. This is especially true when the small business owner does not have the funds to pay back family or friends.

When I am coaching small businesses and the discussion of Friends and Family arises, I ask them the question, "Can you handle looking across the table at Thanksgiving and telling them that they won't be getting their money back?"

Banks & Credit Unions

Banks and credit unions are sometimes conservative with the risk they are willing to take with small businesses, especially immediately after the economic meltdown of 2008. However, small/local banks and credit unions that are committed to local communities and interested in developing the local economy are generally going to be much more likely to loan you money than large, national banks. These small banks are built on personal relationships.

Some of the key benefits of using banks and credit unions are that they can often provide lower interest rates than other lenders, they don't require any equity, and they tend to have higher customer satisfaction than that of online lenders.

Source: Federal Reserve 2017

Interview: Jim Caldwell, First Citizens Bank

An example of a highly successful community bank is First Citizens Bank in Whitewater, Wisconsin. The bank began in 1863 and has survived the Great Depression, the 2008 economic collapse, technological upheavals in the banking sector, and more. This bank really knows how to survive a crisis!

I interviewed Jim Caldwell, their CEO, to gain his insights on how his bank is navigating the current crisis.

"Our customers do a great deal of their banking online and through our drive through but many seeking mortgages, and small businesses that need our help want to come in and meet with our staff. We shut-down all our bank lobby when the stay-at-home order (for the Coronavirus pandemic) came through here in Wisconsin. But we still had customers that needed help and we made a commitment to continue to pay our employees. We had staff that was working from home but some did not have broadband Internet available and others didn't have fast computers. So, we immediately connected broadband service where available, regardless of price, and purchased computers for our employees. Our customers were happy because we didn't miss a beat...they still received the personal customer service they expect, and our employees are happy because they continued to get their salaries and received the tools they needed at no charge to help our customers."

Community Development Financial Institutions (CDFIs)

CDFIs are private financial institutions dedicated to providing loans to help residents start and promote businesses, assisting families with financing their first homes and investing in local health centers, schools, or community centers.

Source: CDFI fund.gov

CDFIs are comprised of community development banks, community development loan funds, and community development venture funds. CDFIs raise capital from individuals and institutions (banks, non-financial institutions (i.e. insurance companies), government, religious institutions, and foundations). There were between 8,000 and 10,000 CDFIs in the U.S. in 2016.

Source: Taking Stock, CDFIs Look Ahead After 25 Years of Community Development Finance.

Lenders to CDFIs (e.g. banks) were struck by the mortgage crisis of 2008, causing both the number of funds channeled into CDFIs and the acceptance rate of applications to decline.

CDFIs have a direct interest in spurring their local economy; they tend to be less averse to risk than individual banks. They also provide a local network of other resources and tend to offer lower interest rates than the traditional market. CDFI application processes can sometimes be lengthy, and depending on the locale and relative economic conditions, funds can be limited.

Crowdfunding

Crowdfunding is the process of raising capital to fund a startup, new product idea, invention, project, literary work, event, or special cause through a web-based campaign on a specific crowdfunding platform. There are four types of crowdfunding platforms: Reward, Equity, Donation, and Debt/Loan. If you decide to venture down the crowdfunding path, you need to match your small business type with the crowdfunding platform you choose.

Types of Crowdfunding Services:

Reward Crowdfunding - A service whereby supporters of the campaign receive a tangible reward. Example: A donor to a Kickstarter campaign for a new solar-powered smartphone might receive a free solar panel for their smartphone.

Equity Crowdfunding - A service whereby supporters (investors) receive equity in the firm they support. Example: An individual invests $10k in a small business on AngelList and they receive a 5 percent equity stake in the company.

Donation Crowdfunding - A service whereby supporters receive the psychological benefit of helping a specific cause or individual. Example: An individual creates a campaign on GoFundMe to raise money for hurricane victims.

Debt Crowdfunding - A service whereby supporters provide loans in return for the loan payment plus interest. Example: Individuals each provide support of $10k on Kiva for a woman launching a pottery business in Africa. Within 24 months, they expect to receive a return of the 10K, plus 8 percent interest.

For our purposes, we will focus on "reward crowdfunding". This type of crowdfunding provides the dual benefit of raising capital and simultaneously creating brand awareness with your crowdfunding campaign. Some platforms provide you the opportunity to make actual sales of your product (such as Kickstarter). This can be a tremendous way to conduct product validation.

Sometimes supporters of reward campaigns perceive themselves to be investors and try to make demands beyond that of receiving the product/service that they ordered. This can lead to tremendous distractions when the small business owner needs to be focused on growing the business. Additionally, creating an effective crowdfunding campaign can take a considerable amount of time. And the time to create the copy (text) for the campaign is just the beginning. The most effective campaigns have powerful, compelling videos to engage the campaign supporter. These can take time and money.

Incidentally, I am a homebrewer and bought the "uKeg" pressurized [beer] growler after watching an entertaining and engaging video by Growlerwerks on Kickstarter. They did not spend a tremendous amount on the campaign, but created a compelling story that developed a tremendous amount of buzz (no pun intended) and yielded over 10,000 backers!

Some crowdfunding services, such as Kickstarter, do not pay out the funds unless you hit your goal. So, setting an achievable goal is very important. Other crowdfunding platforms, such as Indiegogo, provide you the funds even if you don't achieve your goal. However, you need to consider the audience before selecting a crowdfunding service. Look at the products and services that are typically promoted on that particular crowdfunding service. More importantly, look at the campaigns that are exceeding their goals and clearly engaging supporters (you can see both a real-time view of the amount of money raised in the campaign and the number of supporters, aka backers).

The fee to use these crowdfunding services typically hovers around 5 percent, but it varies. This fee can be an important consideration if you are seeking to raise a great deal of money, and should be added to the amount you need to receive from the campaign itself.

Restart Insight: Not all crowdfunding services provide you your funds unless you hit your goal. Be sure to set a realistic target.

Online Lending

Not to be confused with crowdfunding, online lending provides loans directly to consumers and businesses. Lenders such as Lending Club, Kabbage, Funding Circle, and OnDeck offer quick and easy loans. These online lenders are, in general, very enthusiastic about funding small businesses (in addition to providing loans to individuals).

Online lending firms tend to have an easy application process and higher acceptance rates vs. traditional funding sources (e.g. banks and credit unions). However, they tend to provide relatively small amounts of capital and tend to charge very high-interest rates.

Angel Investors

Angel investors are usually high net-worth individuals or consortiums of high net-worth individuals.

Interestingly, geography often determines the amount an angel investor is willing to provide. For example, in the U.S. Midwest, a general rule of thumb is that angel investors invest under $1 million. On the West or East Coasts, that number can move up to as much as $3 million. Once you get higher than those amounts, you typically move into venture capital or private equity investments.

There are two distinct types of angel investors relative to their ability to provide strategic guidance.

> **Dumb money** - Individuals or small groups of individuals who possess the capital to invest but do not possess domain expertise in your particular target market, product, or service. The advantage of "dumb money" is that this type of money is much easier to find than "smart money."
>
> Note: If you are trying to ensure you'll never get money from these people, refer to them as "dumb money." The following statement would be a bad idea: *"You know we are really looking for smart money, but we can't find any, so we will take dumb money. When can we pick up the check?"*
>
> **Smart money** - Individuals or, more commonly, consortiums of high net-worth individuals that focus on a specific sector. They possess domain expertise and only invest in that sector/domain.

Venture Capitalists

Venture capital is an investment made by a group of accredited investors in exchange for equity. These investors either contribute through a fund or through a firm. Venture capitalists tend to invest in early-stage companies (post-small business phase) whereas Angel investors typically invest in startups. As a result, venture capitalists tend to invest more capital than angel investors.

Investors in venture capital funds are typically very large institutions, such as pension funds, financial firms, insurance companies, and university endowments—all of which put a small percentage of their total funds into high-risk investments. They expect a return of between 25-35 percent per year over the lifetime of the investment. Because these investments represent such a tiny part of the institutional investors' portfolios, venture capitalists have a lot of latitude. What leads these institutions to invest in a fund is not the specific investments, but the firm's overall track record, the fund's "story," and their confidence in the partners themselves.

Where venture money plays an important role is in the next stage of the innovation life cycle—the period in a company's life when it begins to commercialize its innovation. It is estimated that more than 80 percent of the money invested by venture capitalists goes into building the infrastructure required to grow the business—in expense investments (manufacturing, marketing, and sales) and the balance sheet (providing fixed assets and working capital).

Venture money is not long-term money. The idea is to invest in a company's balance sheet and infrastructure until it reaches a sufficient size and credibility so that it can be sold to a corporation, or so that the institutional public-equity markets can step in and provide liquidity. In essence, the venture capitalist buys a stake in a small business owner's idea, nurtures it for a short period of time, and then exits with the help of an investment banker.

Source: How Venture Capital Works, Bob Zider, Harvard Business Review

Grants

The Technology Program Office, which is part of the Small Business Administration (SBA), administers the Small Business Innovation Research (SBIR) Program and the Small Business Technology Transfer (STTR) Program. Through these two competitive programs, SBA ensures that the nation's small, high-tech, innovative businesses are a significant part of the federal government's research and development efforts. Eleven federal departments participate in the SBIR program; five departments participate in the STTR program, awarding collectively $2 billion to small high-tech businesses each year.

Source: SBA.gov, 10/1/1

Step 5 – Selecting Powerful Small Business Software

The days of needing sophisticated, expensive software that requires days of training and made you want to pull your hair out are long gone.

Most software that small businesses utilize today are sold on a SaaS (Software as a Service) basis. Most SaaS companies provide small businesses the option to pay on a monthly subscription fee instead of large up-front costs. This allowed small businesses to afford software previously only available to large businesses.

Here are some small business software options that I've consistently seen successful small businesses use and that have been positively reviewed.

Software for the Small Business

Our Selection Criteria:

- **Affordable:** They tend to have freemium (free options) and premium options that are provided on a monthly subscription price basis.
- **Powerful:** They tended to have most of the functionality that a small business requires. However, custom and specialized software will be needed by some small businesses.
- **User-Friendly:** They can be set-up by the small business itself without specialized training and without paid customization.

Accounting	Quickbooks, Freshbooks
Cloud Storage	Box, Google Drive, Dropbox
Communications	Slack, Gmail, Basecamp
Customer Service	Freshdesk, Zendesk
Ecommerce	Shopify, Squarespace, Weebly
G-Suite (All in one software from Google)	Google Docs, Google Drive, Google Slides, Google Sheets, Gmail, Google Calendar, Google Meet
Inventory Management	Fishbowl, Shopify, Square
Marketing	Hubspot, SproutSocial
Project Management	Basecamp, Monday, Trello
Sales Management	Hubspot, Pipedrive, Zoho
Webinars	GoToMeeting, WebEx, Zoom
Website Builder	GoDaddy, Square, WIX, WordPress

Below is software that I find many small businesses aren't using but can have almost immediate positive impacts on small businesses.

GoDaddy – Quickly secure website addresses, hosting, website builder tools and email addresses. This is an easy one-stop-shop to save time and money.

Slack – Improves internal company communications over email through group messaging, direct messaging, and organizing teams.

Shopify – Quickly and easily build out a basic Ecommerce site including integrated payment processing.

Sprout Social – Efficiently social media management planning and insights with powerful reporting.

Trello – Saves time and money when managing complex projects.

ZenDesk – Improvement management of customer service operations.

Step 6 – Growing Small Business Ecommerce Sales

Ecommerce

Whether your company is a B2B (Business-to-Business), B2C (Business-to-Consumer), or B2G (Business-to-Government) and regardless of whether you are selling products or services, Ecommerce is an important piece of a successful small business model. Do not skip this chapter because you assume that Ecommerce has no role to play in your small business!

This chapter contains a number of interviews with highly successful small and large business owners and these conversations will illustrate how critical Ecommerce has become for every sized business.

The What and Why Behind Ecommerce

The worldwide expansion of the Internet has considerably contributed to the transformation of trade and store transactions. Ecommerce, or electronic commerce, largely means buying and/or selling products through the internet and is commonly associated with online shopping. Ecommerce also makes use of regular technological maintenance to ensure the smooth functioning of online store sites, monetary transactions, as well as everything to do with providing and delivering products.

There are several different types of Ecommerce, the most prevalent being B2B (business-to-business), B2C (business-to-consumer) and C2C (consumer-to-consumer) Ecommerce. Furthermore, mobile commerce in the shape of buying and selling goods and content via mobile devices such as smartphones is also on the rise.

Mobile commerce growth is another exciting trend to watch in terms of Ecommerce statistics, considering the popularity and widespread use of smartphones and the growing usage of tablets. This type of Ecommerce includes mobile media and content, retail services, travel purchases, and various other services.

Digital payments are also closely connected to Ecommerce. Alternative payment methods such as digital wallets or online payment providers have seen increased adoption rates and rapid growth in the past few years. Digital payments are not only convenient for the mobile shopping experience but also for the increasingly available paid digital content like streaming music, online video subscriptions, and apps.

In 2019, retail Ecommerce sales worldwide amounted to 3.53 trillion US dollars and e-retail revenues are projected to grow to 6.54 trillion US dollars in 2022. Online shopping is one of the most popular online activities worldwide.

Statista website, Statistics, and Data about Ecommerce, June 2019

How Do You Know if Your Ecommerce Efforts are Effective?

Ecommerce Metrics:

1. Impressions.
2. Reach.
3. Engagement.
4. Email click-through-rate.
5. Cost per acquisition (CPA).
6. Organic acquisition traffic.
7. Social media engagement.
8. Abandonment.
9. Micro to macro conversion rates.
10. Average order value (AOV).
11. Sales conversion rates.
12. Customer Retention rate.

13. Customer lifetime value (CLV).
14. Repeat customer rate.
15. Refund and return rate.
16. Ecommerce churn rate.
17. Net promoter score (NPS)
18. Subscription rate
19. Program participation rate.

Impressions - Simply put, impressions are the number of times your ad or piece of content is presented to someone. Those impressions can occur via paid ads on third-party sites, search results, social platforms, etc. (anywhere, really).

Impressions are one of the most controllable metrics you can have, as they're almost entirely based on the budget you allocate to your various activities.

Reach - Put plainly, reach is the total number of your followers and subscribers — basically, the sum of all of those who will see your content. This might include your email opt-in subscribers, your Facebook followers, and your loyalty program subscribers.

Reach is best improved by consistent campaigns (social media, email, or otherwise) to encourage subscribers, followers, etc. The better defined your brand and voice are, the more effective your campaigns will be to improve reach.

Engagement - Engagement is the intersection of your Impressions and your reach. Essentially: how many of your followers and subscribers (your reach) are engaging with your content (your impressions). This may include acquisition-related activities like click-through, but it may also include non-acquisition-related activities such as likes and shares.

Engagement will most benefit from CONTINUED activities to promote your brand and product. It's important to make these efforts in a continuous fashion. These efforts are much more like farming (ongoing) than they are hunting (one-off).

You can't have a buyer if they don't get to your site. Now that they're aware of your brand, let's define some metrics that measure getting them to your site. There are many, many metrics in this phase of the funnel, so we'll only focus on a few.

Email click-through - Email click-through rate is how many of your email subscribers (who've received the email AND opened it, which are other metrics) clicked through to your site.

You can positively impact this by creating well-designed emails (including mobile-friendly design), strong calls-to-action, and good subject lines.

Cost per acquisition (CPA) - Do you think it'd be helpful to know how much you're paying for acquiring your customers (or your CAC, customer acquisition cost)? We'll take that as a yes, which is why it's important to make sure that you're not launching exorbitant campaigns that produce only a small number of customers.

As a store owner, you know you're going to have to invest in email campaigns, paid search campaigns, and other marketing investments in order to drive traffic and, ultimately, sales. But if the cost of those campaigns outweighs the total revenue they're generating, then you're making poor use of your all-important dollars.

Your CPA can be improved by segmenting your campaigns to better target customers who will best respond to your campaigns' call-to-actions, landing pages that will help reinforce your call-to-actions, and managing your campaign budgets carefully.

Organic acquisition traffic - In the long run and in a blue sky, you hope to attract people to your site without paying for them. It follows that it's important to measure how many of your visitors reach the site organically, which is commonly available in all analytics platforms.

You can improve your organic traffic by ensuring that your on-site/technical SEO remains true to best practices (proper tagging, good response time, etc.) and that your off-page SEO performs well (which rings back to some of the concepts in the discovery section of this blog).

Social media engagement - Social media metrics can provide a lot of value to your Ecommerce company. These are the top social media engagement KPIs you should track on a regular basis:

- Likes per post: "Likes" is a catch-all metric I am using for people that have upvoted your social media posts. These will come in the form of Likes, thumbs-ups, favorites, or +1's. To calculate it, you will need to collate likes on each social media platform and divide it by the number of posts on the individual platform.
- Shares per post: "Shares" is a catch-all metric for "shares," "retweets" and "repins." This metric is indicative of the average number of times posts are shared over a given amount of time.
- Comments per post: "Comments" is a catch-all metric for mentions and comments to your social media posts. This metric is a gauge of how much of a community your brand is garnering on social media.
- Clicks per post: The clicks per post metric measures link click-throughs from social media posts over a given time period. To calculate this metric, collate the number of clicks from your social media posts over a specific period (typically over a month) and then divide it by the number of published social media posts over the same time period.

3. Conversion metrics.

Now that you're lucky enough to have a visitor to your store, how can you measure your performance in converting them from a store visitor to a paying customer, adding products to their shopping cart, and actually checking out? These metrics should help you do just that.

Shopping cart abandonment rate - Abandonment can be measured in a few different ways, which is helpful to measure site behaviors. Shopping cart abandonment is a measure of how many people add something to their cart but LEAVE your site WITHOUT making a purchase. This measure is important to see if there are hitches in the site or cart process before they get to the checkout process.

Checkout abandonment - Separately, checkout abandonment is a critical metric of how many people leave your site WITHOUT making a purchase BUT ONLY AFTER they begin the checkout process. While similar to shopping cart abandonment, it's important to measure them separately to see if the checkout process is the root cause of abandonments or if the problem is something else entirely.

Your abandonment rates can be improved primarily by intuitive cart management, which includes persistent pages, urgency messaging, saving customers carts, etc.

These are similar to the abandonment rates but can give you an opportunity to measure activities you consider important to your funnel, such as the number of visitors who click to a product detail page, or the number of visitors who opt-in as an email subscriber.

Average order value (AOV) - Your AOV is the average price your customers are paying for the items in their cart when they check out. It can, and should, be measured over time, so you can determine how it evolves. It's an important measurement to know as it relates to measurements of marketing effectiveness.

Your AOV can be increased by selling add-ons, loyalty programs, or other, more fundamental business model questions like pricing, product quality, etc.

Sales conversion rates - This is the total number of sales divided by the total number of sessions to your store.

Understanding this number is critical to determining how much traffic is required to generate your target sales.

That said, just like your sales data, you need to more granularly understand conversion rates.

Here are key ways to dissect your conversion rate metric:

- Set conversion rate by channel: e.g. AdWords, SEO, Facebook, etc.
- Set conversion rate by category of products: Some categories may have higher conversions than others
- Set conversion rate by campaign: As an example, if you are working with affiliates or influencers
- Aim to optimize your sales conversion rates in your campaigns. If you have a channel or category performing well, think about putting more behind it, if something is underperforming, maybe there's a fix that would boost the rates, or maybe the campaign should be terminated (sometimes it's best to cut your losses). Conversion Rate Optimization (CRO) can really maximize growth for a campaign.

Retention metrics. - Depending on the source, acquiring a new customer is anywhere from 5 to 25 times more expensive than retaining an existing one. Regardless of the exact amount, the data pretty strongly indicates the value in retaining those customers you've converted.

Note that each of these retention-focused metrics will benefit from a common theme — good customer service, loyalty programs, repeat purchase campaigns, and a true investment in customer satisfaction.

Customer Retention rate - Retention rate is best defined as the percentage of customers you maintain as customers over a period of time. The higher this number, the better you're doing in servicing your customers. It's important to remember to subtract your NEW customers from the customer count when calculating this. Those new customers are important, but this metric is focused on how well you're retaining existing customers.

Customer lifetime value (CLV) - CLV is the total amount you earn from your customers over the length of their relationship with you, as measured by AOV, repeat transactions, and retention period. This is important to calculate, as it's a number to measure to your AOV (hopefully with a significant difference) and can unearth underperforming repeat and retention activities.

Repeat customer rate - This is easy to measure but important to do so. You want to know what percentage of your customers have made multiple purchases. This is another way to measure how well you're servicing your customers because if you're servicing them well, they'll be back.

Refund and return rate - Refund and return rates can be a plague for Ecommerce websites. Even high revenue online stores can be ultimately be done in by high refund and returns. Depending on your industry, returns might be highly common and already baked into your financial models, or alternatively, they may be extremely rare.

Returns can also be a powerful driver to entice customers to hit 'buy now'. If a customer knows your store offers free returns or exchanges, it can alleviate worries about buyers' remorse. Use returns and refunds as fuel to drive your business, not to burn you.

Either way, tracking these metrics are important to the health of your store. Is your refund rate spiking on a specific section of your store? It might be time to investigate where that's coming from.

Ecommerce churn rate - Churn rate is a metric to track the turnover of your customers. It measures the number of users lost over a given period of time. Depending on your industry and sales approach, you may have a long investment time into each user but they stay with you for years, our customers come in easily but they don't seem to stay forever. Whatever your churn rate is, it's important to measure and work on strategies to delight your customers when they're around. It's always easier to resell to a current customer than to gain a new one.

Net promoter score (NPS) - As recent adoptees ourselves, we're fans of this simple metric: how likely would your customers be to refer you? Based on their numeric answer, customers fall into one of three categories — detractors, passives, and promoters. The more promoters you have, the better (you guessed it).

It's important to note that different industries have different scales of good and bad NPS scores.

Your NPS will benefit from the combination of everything in your business, from your product quality to your customer service quality, from the customer experience you provide to the quality of the employment experience you offer your employees. NPS measures everything and is incredibly valuable to measure.

Subscription rate - As email marketing remains high-value, it's important to know what percentage of your visitors have opted-in for your email lists. This signals that your customers WANT to hear from you. And that's obviously a good thing.

Your subscription rate can be improved by ensuring a good email communication experience (know your brand, be consistent in messaging, don't "spam" your list with endless or unnecessary messages), an easy subscription experience, and strong calls-to-action.

Program participation rate - As Ecommerce technologies and practices have matured, more and more merchants have turned to advocacy programs like loyalty programs or review platforms. There are numerous solutions in both of those realms, but let's use loyalty programs as an example, which may be more pertinent to you if you are a more brand-intensive merchant.

If you have a customer loyalty program, what percentage of your customers are members of it? The higher that percentage, the greater your ability to treat them with care, make them feel special, and improve many other metrics we've discussed, such as CLV, repeat customers, etc.

Conclusion

Operating a successful Ecommerce store requires your attention in a number of ways — from building your store to defining your brand, to creating your product, to offering high-quality customer service.

Familiarity with the Ecommerce metrics mentioned above will help you identify how well you're performing those activities, and highlight those areas in which you can fine-tune your strategies and tactics to improve your store's performance and bottom line. Good luck, and remember to take care of those customers.

BigCommerce, Which Ecommerce statistics should you measure and why, May 2020

Interview: Liz Oh, Levi Strauss and Company

Liz Oh, has over 20 years in retail including merchandising and Ecommerce including her roles at Amazon as Divisional Merchandise Manager of Women's Apparel, at The North Face as the Director of Ecommerce Merchandising and her current role as Director of Merchandising, Ecommerce and Mainline Stores for Levi Strauss and Company.

I wanted Liz to share her insights into "omnichannel retailing." Omnichannel retailing is the concept of selling your products through the sales channels and technologies where and when your customers want to buy. For example, your customers might want to buy from your retail location in Chicago, or from their smartphone when they are traveling, or from the convenience of their laptop at home.

I asked Liz to share her insights into how having an omnichannel retail strategy is important for small businesses.

"Omnichannel retailing is a necessity for survival in today's retail landscape for all retail businesses including small businesses. The mantra for this concept is how to make shopping easier and frictionless for your customer. It's also about making your inventory productive and accessible to your consumer wherever they are.

Consumers are shopping on their phones much more frequently than over the desktop or laptops. Therefore, it's mandatory that you prioritize your mobile site with fast load times, ease of navigation, and frictionless checkout. Sometimes we want to over complicate the digital user experience, which leads to slower load times and a frustrated customer. Simplify and prioritize speed for a more positive experience.

For navigation, the hamburger (three horizontal lines signifying the menu) needs to be in an intuitive location. Often the upper right-hand corner. Prioritize onsite search also making search highly visible. It's all about helping the consumer get to the desired product with the fewest number of clicks. Autofill in your checkout creates a frictionless checkout and a happier consumer. If you're thinking about creating an app, that's great, but make sure your website is mobile-friendly before you create an app.

Once you've nailed your mobile site experience with a frictionless consumer experience it's time to ensure you're leveraging inventory across channels. Having multiple bricks [retail brick and mortar] locations and a website with segregated inventory can lead to unproductive inventory and disappointed customers. Those disappointed might decide that they never want to buy from your small business again. Leveraging that inventory across channels is critical. The pandemic put an exclamation point on this necessity. Having the ability to fulfill orders from both Ecom (Ecommerce)warehouses and store inventory, while stores were closed, eased pressure on warehouses with reduced capacity to fill orders, and prevented dead inventory in stores during closures. Even without the pandemic, there are times when you might sell out of an item in one pool of inventory and need to leverage another pool to fulfill consumer demand. Shipping Ecom orders from store inventory need to be seamless to the consumer. To the customer, all they see is that they have placed an online order. It doesn't matter to them where you've shipped it from."

Another way to leverage omnichannel inventory is to buy online pick up in-store from store inventory (BOPIS). It's again about making shopping easier for the customer. Whether the customer needs it right away and doesn't want to wait (or pay) for shipping, or they want the security of the product not sitting on their doorstep with the risk of theft. This functionality has also been key during the pandemic as the economy gradually opened to allow curbside pickup, BOPIS, which made this experience frictionless.

The final way to leverage omnichannel inventory is serving the customer is in the location of your brick from Ecommerce inventory. Let's face it having a compelling assortment in your stores means an edited POV (point of view) within space constraints. Offering color or style extensions on your website is called "the long tail' assortment strategy."

Interview: Ryan Breslow, Bolt

Next, I wanted to illustrate the importance of having a user-friendly Ecommerce experience for customers. For this, I turned to Ryan Breslow, the Founder, and CEO of Bolt. Bolt is a fascinating, rapidly growing FinTech (Financial Technology) company based in San Francisco that specializes in Ecommerce. I asked Ryan to share his story, the story behind Bolt, how the Bolt technology works, and lessons for small businesses when it comes to maximizing their Ecommerce sales.

"Even at a young age, I was fascinated by payments and how money is handled. Back in high school and college, I helped businesses set up their Ecommerce websites and it was during this time that I realized there was a big problem: merchants were losing customers at the finish line. The checkout process was extremely high friction, and I realized that even though there were a lot of tools that touched checkout (payment, fraud, cart, tax, coupons, etc..), there was not a single company who was bringing the pieces together holistically to drive an elegant customer experience. My interest in solving this problem continued when I went to Stanford, and in 2014 I decided to drop out to create Bolt and pursue my vision for the future of online payments.

I'm passionate about leveling the Ecommerce playing field by giving retailers a simple, seamless, safe, mobile-optimized checkout experience. Prior to founding Bolt, I spent six years building Ecommerce sites for businesses of all sizes — from small mom and pop shops to large corporations. It was during this time that I experienced first-hand the shortcomings of the online commerce space, which inspired me to design a better alternative. Since then, we've reached $1 billion in annualized payments revenue, and have powered millions of online checkouts.

The key to Bolt's success really comes down to its ability to take something as complex as checkout and make it easy for retailers to integrate into their backend. Many online retailers use different software to enable checkout, adding complexity and time for the customer. By powering checkout as a platform, Bolt helps retailers lower their overhead and drive newfound revenue. This ultimately helps them compete in a world where Amazon's one-click checkout dominates. That's why our mission is simple: to level the playing field. Bolt streamlines checkout and handles the tech for businesses so that they can focus on building their brand and product. We help create a better experience for shoppers by helping retailers lower the cost of overhead, increase revenue through higher conversion rates, and increase security.

Small businesses looking to grow their Ecommerce successes should invest in technology that makes the customer experience as delightful as possible. Don't reinvent the wheel, instead find an existing solution that works well and run with it. This will not only save businesses time and resources, but it will also allow them to focus on building better products and fostering customer relationships.

Lastly, Dave, I wanted to share a story for your readers about a retailer based in Kansas. All Things Barbecue, a Wichita-based retailer offering equipment, sauces, rubs, and accessories needed for cooking outdoors, is an example of a company that has grown using Bolt. Prior to partnering with Bolt, the company was having issues with cart abandonment at checkout, customers were being declined to false positives, and they had zero protection from fraud. Since switching to Bolt, the company has seen a 190% increase in checkout conversion, an abandoned cart rate under 50%, and a 60% increase in order approval rate. And in just under a year working with Bolt, All Things Barbecue reported 6-digit increases in month-over-month revenues."

The last major consideration for maximizing Ecommerce that we will cover in this chapter is working WITH Amazon and handling warehousing and logistics. Amazon can be a powerful and incredibly profitable partner.

Interview: Jeff Peterson, Geneva Supply Company

Jeff Peterson is the CEO and Co-Founder of Geneva Supply, a company that provides comprehensive marketing, warehousing, and logistics for businesses that want to outsource their Ecommerce distribution. Geneva Supply has been featured in Entrepreneur magazine, selected as a Future 50 company, and the founders, Jeff and his business partner, Mark Becker, have been named Small Business Administration "Persons of the Year." Jeff also developed and runs a program called BizTank that provides one-of-a-kind business opportunities for high school students to engage with business leaders and work on real-world projects.

I asked Jeff to discuss Ecommerce warehousing and logistics. He started the conversation with an important mindset shift that many small businesses need to make.

"I want to make one first point that is critical for small businesses to understand. Many small businesses see Amazon solely as a huge competitive threat. But the small businesses that thrive actually capitalize on Amazon's platform. They need to change their mindset and use Amazon to generate more business. For example, you can create your own online store within Amazon's platform, your Seller Central microsite. So, your products are not listed next to your competitor's products. If you are not using this service and your competitors are then you are missing out on business. If you are concerned about the negative impact then just test it out, run a pilot, and see if it has a positive impact on your business.

As Amazon makes it easier for sellers to utilize their platform as an open Marketplace, the rest of the Ecommerce channels are following suit. So, before you spend all of your money thinking you need to do it all on your own, learn how each Marketplace is set up to help you in a well-rounded strategy.

If you are a manufacturer these days it is very risky to just rely on a wholesaler to be your only channel of distribution. If you think about the end customer that just wants a good quality product, as quickly as they can then having another step between you, the manufacturer, and your customer just doesn't make sense anymore. Many of these wholesalers are just putting your products next to all of the competitors in their catalog or website that they represent anyway. They aren't really differentiating you. So, why not take control into your own hands? Yes, you will create channel disruption, you might even lose your whole dealer network. Here is the thing, "that channel is probably going away anyway and they are already and your products are already being shopped against other products.

Whether you are a manufacturer or a retailer, Ecommerce has changed your business forever you know it or not and there is no going back. You only need to look at the recent bankruptcies of retailers to see that trend.

The Coronavirus epidemic has just accelerated that change. If your business was deemed non-essential your business was shut-down, just shut-down like that [snapped his fingers]. There will be companies that will literally go out of business because they either didn't have an Ecommerce presence or that presence was completely ineffective.

I think another important point that we make with our clients is that they must not rely on only one sales channel. We do a tremendous amount of business with Amazon but also represent 66 other Ecommerce firms as well. We don't think that any company should even just rely on Amazon. It is no different than having one supplier, one customer service person, one salesperson, or one customer. At some point, a problem is going to occur, and the wheels come off the bus. Look at businesses deemed as essential vs. non-essential. If you didn't have a second way to sell your products in addition to Amazon your product shipment dates were going to get delayed. Customers want things now. So, if you didn't have your own Ecommerce site or a second third party company, like Geneva Supply that represents many Ecommerce platforms then you could be out of business.

Businesses that truly want to thrive need to look at their Ecommerce strategies, talk with the end customer and ask what they want, *consider eliminating a wholesaler network, and build out a robust Ecommerce strategy.*

As Amazon makes it easier for sellers to utilize their platform as an open Marketplace, the rest of the Ecommerce channels are following suit. So, before you spend all of your money thinking you need to do it all on your own, learn how each Marketplace is set up to help you in a well-rounded strategy."

Restart Insight: *Many small businesses see Amazon solely as a huge competitive threat. But the small businesses that thrive capitalize on Amazon's platform. They need to change their mindset and use Amazon to generate more business.*

Step 7 – Building the Ultimate Small Business Team

Growing from a Team of One

If you decide to create a "lifestyle" business, where your primary goal is to maintain a specific standard of living, you can keep your organization very small—maybe even only a team of one. Some examples of lifestyle businesses would include a small consulting firm, a small accounting practice, a small insurance office, a plumber, a manufacturers rep, a dentist's office, a law practice, a small retail store, a niche Ecommerce store, or a marketing firm. Keep in mind that without a marketing department, sales team, accounting department, operations, engineering, and administrative teams, and a vendor network, these tasks and operations are all your responsibility when you're a one-person business. Typically, successful lifestyle businesses will eventually need to hire some employees.

One thing I've learned from my own small business is the ability to assess my strengths and weaknesses. I went from participating in traditional leadership surveys, where only my employees evaluated me, to 360-degree feedback assessments. During my career as a manager working for Fortune 500 firms, I was accustomed to regular leadership reviews that provided solid guidance.

When I was in sales, I was a good, consistent performer (received 12 Pacesetter Awards at BellSouth, sold the first wireless PBX, developed a sales territory from five clients to over 1,500 clients, etc.). In marketing, where I managed up to $20 million-per-year marketing budgets, I almost always achieved our targets, managed marketing through thousands of sales agents, and nearly always came in under budget. I learned some very valuable sales, marketing, and management insights that I knew would hold me in good stead. I understood my strengths.

However, these successes didn't help me identify weaknesses or gaps in knowledge that became quickly and painfully apparent when I was building my small business. Although I had received accolades for leadership and awards for sales performance, I was never responsible for cash flow management; I didn't have to engage in complex projects; I wasn't involved in overseeing software development; I didn't have to work with investors; I didn't lead a board of directors. Successful small businesses possess the ability to learn from mistakes, acquire critical new knowledge, and combine those to develop new skills that lead their small business to success.

Management Lesson from Cancun

I launched my first small business, Sales Sherpas, as a team of one. I landed a $20,000 sale that was designated as a "marketing research" project. The project turned out to be making thousands of cold calls for a telecom company, which was not what I expected but the money was good. I put my sales skills to good use and I was off and running. However, while I was focused on actually doing the work itself, I had not dedicated enough time to filling "the pipeline" with new work or new clients. At my corporate jobs, I had other people creating and delivering the products and services that I marketed and sold. Now, I was wearing a sales hat and an operations hat. The inevitable occurred; I finished up with the $20,000 project, and although I had "deals in the pipeline," none of them had closed. I landed some small marketing projects, a couple of $5,000 deals, and $10,000 deals and really started to get back into "sales mode."

Financially, I hadn't yet reached the level of income I had provided for my family when I was in corporate, but I was doing well enough to go on a family vacation to Cancun.
Being from Wisconsin, my family and I are, naturally, diehard Packers fans (Bears fans, please do not set fire to this book or destroy your smartphone or computers). While we were in Cancun, a Packers vs. Bears game was being televised but we

couldn't access it on the TV in our hotel room. I frantically called around to find somewhere to watch the game and the only place showing it was a chain restaurant with a reputation for great chicken wings and female servers in rather tight-fitting clothes. I had promised my six-year-old son we would see the game and, of course, no self-respecting Packers fan would miss a game against the Bears so I told my wife that my son and I were headed to a "local restaurant" to watch the big event.

No sooner had we settled in to enjoy the game when my cell phone rang. It was a prospect I had been working with for months. I had been pitching Sales Sherpas to replace their incumbent advertising agency that wasn't getting results. Because of the game and the crowd, there was a significant amount of noise in the background. I told the prospect that I was sorry about the noise and that it was "my son's birthday party," but I could take a few minutes for him. I'm happy to say that the Packers won that night and I landed the deal.

But the story is not over. I got back to the hotel and told my wife about the deal - Sales Sherpas biggest to date and one that would guarantee more financial security for my family - and, while she showed more relief than excitement, I understood that she was genuinely happy for me. Then I told my son to "tell mom about the Packers game." He exclaimed, "Well mommy, we went to this place to watch the Packers, and all these girls had really short shorts!" Let's just say that my wife's relief and happiness were slightly tempered by disdain for my choice of venue.

Our family still jokes about that story to this day. When I reflect, the elation I felt at closing that first, big deal, and the lesson I learned about wearing so many hats when you're a small business owner are the ones I carry with me. You can't just focus on operations and product development and forget about sales. You must keep that sales pipeline full. I also realized that I couldn't do it all myself and that I needed to be focusing on sales, and this new deal would require me to hire my first employee. As much as I didn't want to take the financial hit of putting someone on the payroll, I knew that it had to happen. It was time to start building a team.

It was painful to cut into my company's cash flow and take on overhead. Now, you are taking money out of your own pocket, away from your family, to pay others. But, eventually, every growing business has to expand its human resources. One person simply can't do it all. I hired my first employee, Carol, to manage relationships with our copywriters, graphic designers, and software developers, and to conduct billing. I hired Carol because she had the ability to be friendly yet firm. I could leave the office for days on trips and know that everything was handled, and I could focus on growing the company.

> **Restart Insight:** *Eventually you will get to the point where you need to acknowledge you can't do it all. You need to go out, make that first hire, and stay focused on growing the business.*

Tips on Building the Best Talent for Your Small Business

It is easy to fall into the trap of hiring friends or people just like ourselves. HR professionals call it the "me too effect." We like to talk with people with similar work experiences, backgrounds and communication styles. So, the natural inclination is to hire those people.

Of course, in traditional corporations, you will find groups of people with similar skills and, frequently, similar communication styles that get hired into specific functional areas. For example, in accounting departments, you tend to get highly analytical people that take the time to prepare thoughtful answers to difficult questions, but they sometimes suffer from "paralysis through analysis." In sales departments, you tend to get highly driven, goal-oriented people who usually are not known for being detail orientated. But you have your VPs, directors, and C-Level teams that coordinate each of those functional areas and theoretically, steer the ship in the right direction.

It is not natural to spend time thinking about your weaknesses or gaps in competencies (knowledge, skills, and abilities) relative to the other functional areas.

Small Business Culture

There is a common misconception that small businesses shouldn't dedicate their time to thinking about culture. But nothing could be further from the truth. Every company, regardless of size, should be clear about the culture they want to foster within their business as it's representative of the brand's mission and vision.

Interview: Aaron Everson, Avid Ratings

Aaron Everson, CEO of Avid Ratings, shared some great insights relative to his experiences at Jellyfish and Shoutlet.

> *"When you are small, you have to find super passionate people. They need to want to put in the extra time and energy that many times aren't required in a regular job. Having the qualifications to do the job is simply not enough. When I am interviewing employees at one of my businesses I ask myself, could I spend all day in a room with this person? If I can't, they are not a good fit.*
>
> *We spent a great deal of time thinking about the culture at Shoutlet. Not just the current culture, but the future culture as well. We looked at things as basic as the paint on the walls. We chose colors that were fun and uplifting. I remember an employee who came up to me one day and said, "I love it here, I don't think I could ever leave." That's the point.*
>
> *The other thing I find is that it takes a conscious effort to define and live a new culture. However, over time it starts to take on a life of its own. One of our employees created a Facebook page called Overheard. It was completely unplanned. The purpose was to share all the funny things that people said at the office. The next thing you know, people were just bursting out laughing randomly during the day. It was great; it reinforced our culture of fun."*

Restart Insight: Define the culture of your company. Hire people you know will live that culture, then watch it manage itself.

Hire Slowly, Fire Quickly

If you want to learn the real importance of the old adage "hire slowly and fire quickly," manage a small business. The temptation to wait until the last minute to hire someone simply because the cash does not exist to hire everyone you need – so, who do you hire first? Then, you hire a person out of desperation to fix an immediate problem (e.g. increase sales, fill in the schedule). If you're lucky you have a really good understanding of their skill sets, they match your needs, perhaps they were referred to you or you worked with them, they have a strong appreciation for the small business roller coaster ride, and they "hit the ground running."

All of these stars rarely align. More often than not, small businesses don't have the luxury of the classic 60- to 90-day big business hiring cycle (from the job posting all the way to an employee's start date). You might have a week or even a few days. So, you hire someone unproven, and you probably don't think about how you will actually get along with this person. You essentially have just married someone after a one-hour first date.

Then problems start to bubble up ... the person might miss a critical deadline, they might come into work late, you find out they don't have the skills they professed during the interview, or you find that you just don't like them as a person. But you decide to gut it out. You don't have the money or time to find someone else. You tell yourself things like, "they will get better," "we will learn to get along."

Before you know it, critical deadlines are missed, customers are angry, sales productivity drops, products don't work, you find an angry comment on your company's Facebook page and you realize this can't go on…You tell the person to "get the heck out—you're fired."

I haven't met anyone in my career who likes to fire people. I know people who have it down to a science, where it was simply a process of their job, like that of any other job. I used to work with the director of HR at a Fortune 500 company who was a genuinely great guy and mentor to me. He was very process-oriented. The company followed the classic corporate "four strikes (aka coaching sessions/write-ups/warnings) and you're out" process. This tried and true method is great if you have other employees to take up the slack and you have the luxury of time to mentor a failing employee. But, even at this company, if there had been an obvious hiring mistake and that mistake became quickly apparent, my friend would have no hesitation telling the manager to skip the protocol and fire the person right away.

There was no point in hoping the person's behavior would improve or that they would magically learn the skills they said they professed during the interview. One of the things my HR friend used to do when he had to fire a high-profile employee was to wear all black. Imagine Johnny Cash in an HR department. Whenever we saw him come into the office in black, we knew some bad stuff was going down and steered clear of him. In the end, it became a running joke in the office.

Restart Insight: *When it becomes apparent a staff person isn't going to work out, you need to fire them right away. Small businesses don't have the luxury of time or money needed to keep someone on who doesn't contribute immediate value to helping the small business survive and thrive.*

Writing a Clear Job Description

Take the time to write a clear job description of the role. It not only helps the applicant understand some of the expectations of the job, but the exercise helps you clarify what you need in the role. Well written job descriptions also create a professional image of your company and make it easier to recruit. Small business job descriptions need to be very results-oriented. You need to set clear expectations and avoid filling the job description with fluff that doesn't indicate the need for immediate results that move your small business forward.

Following is a job description from one of my small businesses for a business development manager (sales) role.

Business Development Manager

The business development manager will be part of a dynamic small business and be responsible for growing and supporting the business.

Responsibilities:
- Become an expert at identifying challenges prospects face, which can be solved with our software solution.
- Generate highly qualified lead opportunities.
- Identify critical influencers and decision-makers within prospect organizations.
- Qualify prospective small and medium business leads.
- Close new business consistently at or above quota level.
- Follow up on inbound and outbound leads.
- Develop marketing, web, and other advertising initiatives.
- Work collaboratively with other marketing team members and software development to execute a sales strategy.
- Work with team members to constantly refine the company's business model to maximize company growth.
- Other responsibilities ... this is a small business, so you need to be flexible.

Requirements:
- Desire and ability to exceed measurable performance goals
- Demonstrated sales successes (preferred)
- Experience working in a small business environment (preferred)
- Demonstrated results of effective teamwork
- Energy, passion, sense of humor
- Superior written and verbal communication skills
- Strong organizational and time management skills

Independent Contractors

One of my businesses, Bungee, had grown to the point that my business partner, Troy, and I were making a reasonable living –
but I still was not making what I did in a corporate job. I was still wearing many hats and Troy was focused on software development.

My responsibilities included marketing, attending trade shows, conducting sales calls, closing sales, creating marketing campaigns for my clients, managing copywriters, meeting with graphic designers, planning trade shows with Salesforce, preparing for investor meetings, following up on late payments, making deposits of client payments, and on and on.

I was working six days a week and sometimes seven. I was getting worn down. I wasn't spending much time with my kids; I was short when talking with my wife; I rarely saw friends, and I wasn't making time for any of my personal escapes (in my house, these are known as the "Big Bs" – Biking, Boating, and Brewing).

I spent Saturdays and sometimes Sundays doing non-revenue generating activity. When you have a B2B business, like Bungee, you want to spend your weekday "primetime" hours working with customers, because that's when they are available. You also need to do the books, process payables (paying all the bills), log all your receipts, deal with taxes, run financial statements, etc. Not only did I despise this part of my small business life, but it was taking away what little time I had with my family. My children were 9 and 7 at the time, and I knew I needed to spend more time with them. I also wanted to get back to having "date nights" with my wife.

I spoke again with my first small business mentor and dear friend of mine, Joe Jeka. Joe had an extremely successful trade show company and retired early. He lived on a gorgeous spot on our lake. Joe knew I was worn down, and I asked him what I should do. His response was very direct:

"Dave, you are killing yourself, you have grown your business where it is cash flowing, but you are working on weekends doing the books, not spending time with your family, and not enjoying any of your hobbies. You have the money; go out and get yourself a bookkeeper."

There wasn't enough work to justify a full-time bookkeeper on staff. So, I decided to go out and find a bookkeeper who would work as an independent contractor. I found Angie, who to this day does bookkeeping for one of my small businesses. I simply set up QuickBooks Online, connected our business bank account to QuickBooks Online, set up invoices to go out electronically, then funds were paid back into QuickBooks Online and deposited directly into our bank account. Angie, our account, and I all have access to the books by simply logging in when we need to.

Why Use Independent Contractors?

Even when a small business has the money to pay employees, they don't have the luxury of hiring the wrong person. Making the wrong hire can be fatal to a small business. Hire the wrong customer service person, and you might not hit a deadline for that critical client. Hire the wrong business development manager and, if they don't hit their sales goals, they could cause you to burn through cash too quickly.
The answer? The independent contractor (sometimes just called a contractor or subcontractor, depending on circumstances).

Contractor: Independent individual or group of individuals who provide services to organizations on a project basis. These people are typically experts in their fields or have the ability to learn the skills necessary to complete a project or achieve a goal in short order.

The benefits of contractors to small businesses are significant:

1. They tend to be very highly motivated (they only get paid when they deliver results).
2. You eliminate the need to take on long-term overhead.
3. You can quickly select them to do work.
4. You can quickly terminate them if they don't accomplish the work assigned.
5. You don't have to pay taxes or benefits.
6. You get the opportunity to see them complete their tasks under a microscope, and if they do a great job, you can offer them a job, thereby reducing the risk of hiring the wrong person.

Common Mistakes with Contractor Classifications

You need to be extremely careful when selecting someone as a contractor when, in fact, they should be classified as an employee. Some businesses try to classify individuals as contractors to avoid paying taxes, workers' compensation insurance, health insurance, or other benefits. This is not only a morally bad practice but could be an illegal one.

In our currently exploding "gig economy," there are many companies accused of operating in a very grey area (e.g. Uber) regarding the people who are gigging for them. The question is whether their hires should be classified as an employee or a contractor. Attorneys are out to protect people who should be classified as employees, ensuring that they are paid appropriately and that they receive benefits. State Departments of Revenue and the IRS want to make sure that companies pay all of their required taxes.

Once a company starts dictating the hours' someone can work, where they work, or if the company provides supplies and equipment, the workers are no longer "generally" deemed contractors, but employees.

Here are the three factors, directly from the IRS, on how to classify people as employees or contractors.

"Facts that provide evidence of the degree of control and independence fall into three categories:

1. **Behavioral**: Does the company control, or have the right to control, what the worker does and how the worker does his or her job?
2. **Financial:** Are the business aspects of the worker's job controlled by the payer (e.g. things like how the worker is paid, whether expenses are reimbursed, who provides tools/supplies, etc.)?
3. **Type of Relationship:** Are there written contracts or employee type benefits (e.g. pension plans, insurance, vacation pay, etc.)? Will the relationship continue, and is the work performed a key aspect of the business?"

Source: Internal Revenue Service website, Oct 2017

Don't try to guess whether a person should be classified as an independent contractor or an employee. You can end up with serious issues with your state and the federal government if you are not paying taxes for someone who should be classified as an employee. Talk with your accountant for guidance.

One of my small businesses selected an independent contractor, Lynn, to be an independent sales agent for us, not a business development person (salesperson). She was not on our payroll and was only paid based on commission. We did not tell her what hours she should work. She invoiced us for the commissions she had earned. She did not have a company computer but would come into our office for weekly sales meetings.

One day we received a "friendly letter" from the Wisconsin Department of Revenue stating that they were conducting an audit into whether Lynn was actually serving as an "independent contractor" or an "employee." When you are busy running a small business, the last thing you want to spend your time on is surprise issues like this. And frankly, a letter like this from a government agency or a lawyer is very stressful if you haven't experienced it before. I had been careful not to cross the line on the employee/contractor issue and we were fine—Lynn was in fact, deemed to be an independent contractor. But the headaches of paperwork, phone calls, and emails were a major distraction. If you do step over the line, you will not only have to deal with this onslaught of distractions from your day-to-day business, but you will also face fines, payments for back taxes, and be placed on a watch list for the future.

If you do select someone as a contractor, it is critical that you develop a contractor agreement. Two critical elements you must include are that the work is "for hire," and that they agree to a non-compete and non-disclosure clause. I have seen many small business founders have a contractor begin work without a contractor agreement. Then the relationship goes sour and the contractor might have proprietary information they could use to launch their own small business (your friendly, new competitor). Also, without an agreement, they could imply you that intended to hire them as an employee, not a contractor.

Talk with your attorney about creating a contractor agreement for your small business.

Restart Insight: *Independent contractors can be a very flexible way to get work accomplished by highly motivated individuals and organizations without taking on overhead. But, make sure you do not classify someone as an independent contractor who should be an employee.*

Step 8 – Creating Small Business Pilots

Over the years, I've seen a lot of great small businesses that have come up with new business models built on solid discovery and research but they never launch. Why? Because the business owner is paralyzed by fear that the new business model will fail in some way. You can overcome this fear by running a pilot.

In this section, we are going to discuss creating plans for betas, pilots, and commercial launches.

Let's begin with some definitions:

Beta testing is when a select group of end-users tries the system under an initial test, before deployment, to provide feedback about the product. The word beta is commonly used by companies that are testing the latest version of their new software.

Pilot testing is done at the client-side (last stages of development cycle), where all end-users use the system to see whether the system is working as per their given requirements.

Many business people do not differentiate between the two, using the terms interchangeably. Frequently, due to demands on time, they are both conducted at the same time. **We are going to be using the term "pilot"** because it is a more generally accepted term amongst small businesses and will be more logical to customers.

Pilots give you the opportunity to run a short-term test on a new business model or idea without making long-term time and capital commitments. If the pilot doesn't work, you can pivot or just move on to the next idea.

There is also an interesting psychological phenomenon around pilots. When I tell people that we are running a pilot or ask someone if they would like to put time or money into a pilot they usually agree. Pilots are considered inherently low(er)-risk. A pilot gives people and companies a way out if the business model or idea doesn't work. It also reduces the stress of the person running the pilot and helps set realistic expectations for customers.

When you ask customers if they would like to participate in the pilot, set expectations (low), create dates for feedback, explain any associated costs for the customer, confirm the length of the pilot, what will happen if the pilot is successful and what will happen if it is not successful. **There is an element of exclusivity when being asked to participate in a pilot too, so you will most likely find that finding customer participants is much easier than you think.**

Interview: Aaron Hirschman, Plas-Tech Engineering

When I was looking for someone to talk about pilots and innovation, I turned to Aaron Hirschman, the President and Founder of Plas-tech Engineering. Plas-tech Engineering provides premium, plastic engineering molding products, and services to the medical, biotech, and pharma industry. Aaron shared his insights on how his manufacturing company stays years ahead of its competition through innovation and piloting new products.

"Dave, our domestic competition just lives in the here and now, frankly they are not very innovative. There are also companies in China and India that just provide commodities there is no value add. Their customers just care about price and it almost always comes back to bite the customer. Some of our best customers have been burned by competitors who come to us and will never leave. They understand the true value that we bring to their businesses.

Our strategic plans are not 1-year plans but 5 years out. We look at where our client's industries are going, we are always listening intently to what our customers are asking for not just as it relates to our current products and services but pain points they are experiencing. Then we brainstorm potential new products and services with them. Then we simply ask them would you pay for this product X or service Y? How much would you pay? If we can help the customer and it makes sense for us then we pilot it, make changes as necessary, and go. Our competition just can't be that nimble. That is one of our significant competitive advantages.

Financial Services is a sector that is traditionally bogged down by regulation and is typically very slow to adopt new technologies and processes. However, some financial services companies are willing to adapt.

Innovation doesn't just exist in the areas of products, services, and software. Even traditional sectors such as insurance and financial services have firms that innovate.

Interview: Tyson Ray, FORM Wealth Advisors

I interviewed Tyson Ray the CEO and Founding Partner at FORM Wealth Advisors – a financial services company that provides retirement, investment, money, insurance, tax, and estate services. He spoke about how his company's flexibility and innovation has seen them through explosive growth as well as the chaos of the pandemic. FORM Wealth Advisors provides retirement, investment, money, insurance, tax, and estate services.

FORM Wealth Advisors has experienced explosive growth and one of the strategies they have employed to drive that growth is always testing new ideas, new processes, and new technology.

"There are not many innovative firms in financial services. Most firms simply provide clients checkboxes, their firms are just on autopilot. We really try to think differently in terms of not just giving our clients what they want but the way it. We are always available to talk to our clients but some clients wanted the information accessible online at any time. So, we created the FORM Wealth Advisors YouTube Channel.

Our clients regularly have questions when the market is up and the market is down. So, we created a video for our YouTube channel as a test and called it "Up or Down." The "Up or Down" video explained what happened in the market that month, why it happened, and what can be done with investments. Our clients loved it so we now have an "Up or Down" series and we create videos each month.

When the Coronavirus began we knew that our clients were rapidly adopting Zoom. We are used to having face-to-face meetings with our clients, they appreciate those. But with the Coronavirus and the stay-at-home orders, those face-to-face meetings were no longer possible so we created Zoom meetings with our clients. We again provided exactly what our clients wanted they wanted while still providing our personal touch."

Testing innovations and new ideas is a great way to set aside the fear of failure. The first thing you need to do is to plan your pilot. This launch plan will provide the guidebook to coordinate the people, money, and other resources necessary to run the pilot. The best way to create a pilot plan is to work backward from a full launch, which will be your next step if the pilot proves successful.

Here are some tips to help you create your plan

1. Engage as many people as possible from different roles in your company in this exercise. This will ensure you don't miss any steps, and that you get buy-in from everyone. You might find critical people or processes left out if you don't include as many as possible
2. Work backward from your full commercial launch date. This is the date when you plan to roll out to the initial market—not your pilot.
3. Move backward from the "full launch date" to your "pilot launch date".
4. Make sure you allow double the amount of time you think you need to make product/service modifications based on the feedback you receive from your pilot.
5. Allow double to triple the amount of time you think you will need for product development unless you have already been through this process with similar products/services and know the amount of time this step will take.
6. Clearly define the goals of your pilot (what do you need to learn?).
7. Hold yourself and others accountable for deliverables and dates. Many of your tasks will be dependent upon the previous task's completion. These previous tasks are referred to as dependencies.
8. Keep the launch plan dynamic and accessible to your team online with a service such as Trello (see Software for the Small Business in the Appendix).

Basic Small Business Pilot Plan:

	01/01/18	02/01/18	03/01/18	04/01/18	05/01/18	06/01/18	06/15/18	07/01/18
Major Milestones								
Beta Launch						TODD		
Beta End							TODD	
Full Commercial Launch								TODD
Software Development								
Launch Beta Sign-Up Page	BILL							
Build User Interface (UI)		BILL	BILL	BILL	BILL			
Make UI Changes Based on Beta Results						BILL	BILL	
Back-End Development		JENNY	JENNY	JENNY	JENNY			
Make Back-End Developed Changes Based on Beta Results						JENNY	JENNY	
Usability Testing							JENNY	
Beta Live								BILL

Sales & Marketing	01/01/18	02/01/18	03/01/18	04/01/18	05/01/18	06/01/18	06/15/18	07/01/18
Telesales Calls to Prospective Customers	FRED	FRED	FRED	FRED	FRED	FRED		
Weekly Website Traffic Analysis (Begins Post Website Home Page Launch)		JOHN	JOHN	JOHN	JOHN	JOHN	DM	
Develop Intro Video		ANNA						
Search Optimize the Website					MARY			
Set-up Marketing Automation Software					MARY			
Promote Videos on Social Media				LYNN	LYNN	LYNN	LYNN	
Recruit DBD (Director of Business Development)		JOHN	JOHN	JOHN	JOHN	JOHN		
Weekly Webinars with Prospects							DBD	
Recruit DM (Director of Marketing)								
Paid Search Campaigns					TODD	TODD		
Tradeshow Management						DM	DM	DM
On-going Sales Efforts						DBD	DBD	DBD
On-going Marketing Efforts						DM	DM	DM

Legal								
File for LLC		TOM						
Create Operating Agreement		TOM	TOM					
Create Terms and Conditions					TOM	TOM		
Create Privacy Policy				TOM				
Finance								
Register for Federal Tax ID			TOM					
Open Bank Account				TOM				
Client Support								
Conduct Beta Planning Meetings				TEAM	TEAM			
Develop Training Materials (Based on Learning from Meetings)				JENNY	JENNY			
Set-up 800 Number and Integrated Chat					BILL			
Provide Tech Support (on-going)							JENNY/ BILL	JENNY/ BILL

Designing an Effective Pilot

Tips on selecting your participating pilot customers (or prospective customers)

1. Ensure the market is representative of your current or desired target market.
2. Select a sample size that is large enough to gather necessary feedback.
3. Provide enough time to gather feedback.
4. Choose a market that cannot be easily impacted (positively or negatively) by outside sources (e.g. competitors, biases from your small business.
5. Select a target market you can rely on to provide you with timely feedback (I would recommend coordinating meetings/calls/webinars to be held at least once a week).

When designing your pilot, it is critical to define the specific objectives you need to achieve.

Sample Pilot Objectives:

1. **Customer usability** - What modifications do you need to make so customers can easily navigate and gain the proposed benefit of your product? What additional details are needed in the instructions?

2. **Product quality** - Does your product survive rigorous usage by customers?

3. **Feature set** - What additional features does your product/service need?

4. **Marketing** - Does your marketing effectively describe the features, functionality, and benefits?

5. **Channels** - Where do your customers want to purchase your product?

6. **Pricing** - How much are customers willing to pay you for your product/service?

7. **Customer service** - How do customers want to receive customer support? Are they willing to pay additional fees for additional support? This is common in the B2B software market.

8. **Competitive advantages** - How does your product/service compare to other products/services they have used? Are there any weaknesses that need to be addressed? Are there any competitive strengths that need to be accentuated in your marketing?

9. **Satisfaction** - What was their overall satisfaction with the product or service?

10. **Future** - Would they like to participate in future pilots? Would they like to be contacted for purchase when you roll out commercially?

Determining the Pilot Length

Simply put, the length of the pilot must be long enough to gather all of the insights needed to modify the business model. We typically see pilots running 4-8 weeks. However, the level of product complexity and demands of the small business frequently affect that range.

The Art of Setting Low Expectations

Our natural inclination as small businesses is to be eternally optimistic. However, when that optimism turns into setting unrealistically high expectations for the pilot, customers get frustrated, employees who initially supported the pilot get disillusioned and your company can lose credibility.

Therefore, the best course of action is to set expectations incredibly low. It reduces stress on yourself, your team members, and can actually increase customer satisfaction when things go better than anticipated.

Setting low expectations can be done by simply delivering a statement at the beginning of the pilot. I often say something like this:

"We appreciate you taking the time to participate in our pilot. We choose you because we value your feedback enough to help us make decisions about our company's future. Please remember this is a pilot, and the purpose is for us to receive your feedback and modify our product/service accordingly so we can offer new products and services to help customers like you. It is important for you and all those participating to know there will be problems and possibly confusion. Our goal will be to fix those problems and address that

confusion during the pilot, but that will not always be possible. We just want to make sure you understand that this is simply the nature of participating in a pilot."

Creating a Feedback Loop

Given that you are requesting time, energy and potentially money from prospective customers to pilot your product or service, it is important that you have a process in place to respond to their feedback in a timely manner (even if you can't make modifications based on that feedback during the course of the pilot). Without this feedback loop, critical insights that you need to gather from your pilot can be lost, which can have catastrophic implications if you roll out and your product/service does not operate as your small business had promised.

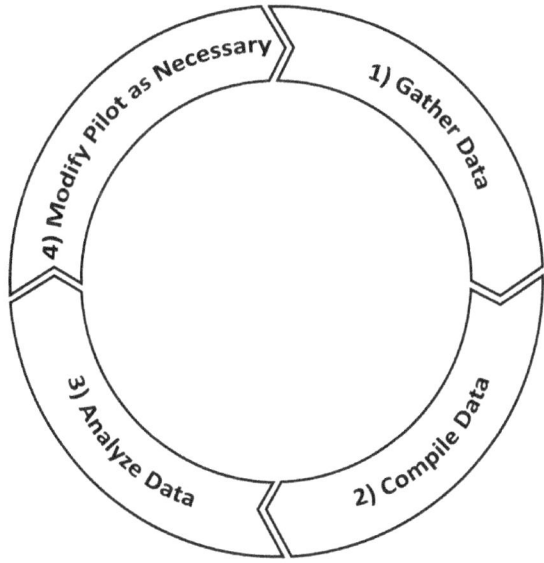

My recommendation is to have frequent meetings, webinars, or calls with pilot users to review participant feedback. At a minimum, provide an interactive way for pilot participants to provide feedback. Frequently, they will have a great number of details to share, and you may have follow-up questions.

I am going old school here and recommend you provide your pilot participants your phone number [gasp]. Pilot participants are not going to want to spend the time taking screen captures, marking them up, and providing written descriptions of the problem in an email or feedback form. If you make the process difficult for them, they will simply not provide you feedback or not enough to ensure you have the information you need to successfully modify your business model/product/service.

Restart Insight: Set low expectations for your pilot customers. It will help the pilot customers understand that things will go wrong and they will be pleasantly surprised if the problems are only minor. Setting expectations low also takes the pressure off you and your team.

Step 9 – Managing Small Business Cash Flow

"Just keep spending until I say stop"

We have all heard the saying, "Cash is king." No one appreciates the critical nature of that statement more than the small business owner. His or her relationship to cash is very different from the one that an employee of a company has where, often, employees can spend company funds with no concern about where the cash came from or where it will come from in the future. For the small business, cash is the lifeblood.

When I was a marketing manager at a Fortune 500 firm (which will remain nameless) just beginning my first week of work, I was beginning to build-out my marketing plan for the year. During the conversation with my marketing director about our sales objectives, I asked about the size of my budget. The response he gave me was, "Just keep spending until I say stop." I wisely watched my money. Unfortunately, others in my department didn't. They ran out of cash in the third quarter and I had enough budget for the entire year.

Established organizations typically have easy access to external sources of cash, including accessing lines of credit, selling stock, issuing bonds, selling inventory, etc. Small businesses can be fragile. Changes in regulations, political parties, technology, economic, and of course competitive factors can rapidly destroy a small business unless they have built-in strategies to thrive.

Small business owners are spinning so many plates when formulating and refining their business model that it is very easy to take their eye off the available amount of cash—especially if that cash is blended with personal bank accounts. Don't let this happen to your small business. Keep a constant eye on your cash and create a separate bank account for your business to separate your finances for accounting and tax purposes. Mixing your business and personal finances, at best, creates confusion for your accountant and, at worst, will yield a visit from a friendly IRS agent.

Restart Insight: Keep a constant eye on your available cash. Cash is the lifeblood of the small business. Separate your personal cash and business cash.

Cash Flow Management 101

For insights on cash flow management, I turned to my colleague and friend, Tim Carr. Tim served as a director at Robert Baird, a wealth management and private equity firm and he has founded multiple small businesses of his own. Tim earned his MBA in Finance from the University of Chicago and now teaches in the Finance, co-directs the Launch Pad (student startup accelerator) and was selected as "Teacher of the Year" in the College of Business and Economics at the University of Wisconsin-Whitewater, in addition to mentoring startups and small businesses.

Tim provided us with the following "crash course" in cash flow management. The sections include explanations of five Cash Flow Traps and how to avoid them.

1. Is your small business funding insufficient?
2. Is your small business funding too much?
3. Will your cash flow support your business?
4. Are your sales estimates, right?
5. Are accounts receivable and accounts payable causing your cash crunch?

After you understand these traps, you will be better prepared to manage your cash flow. Then we will discuss prioritizing how your cash gets spent.

Cash Flow Traps

1. Is Your Small Business Funding Insufficient?

You know what options are available to continue to fund your existing business but what if you want to change your business model in order to thrive? You might want to: open new locations; hire new employees; invest in new technology; order new products; launch more marketing efforts. These are all appropriate "thrive" actions if you have the cash.

Depending on the type of business you have or are going into, your small business funding can differ significantly. If you are setting up a retail store, you may have to consider the time to remodel or do a buildout. Every business will need to consider the time necessary for customers to find you, to acquire repeat customers, and to reach cash flow to stabilize above the "break-even" point while paying yourself, not just your other employees.

With more capital-intensive industries, there will be a longer lead time. Often, three years or more. And, depending on your sector, you may have product development time that extends your time to market and, by extension, cash flow. You don't need all of the funding Day 1 for these companies, though you need enough money to get your business to the next major milestone. It's important to have more capital than you think you need, in case it takes you longer than expected to get there. When you get to that next milestone, various funding doors should start to open. All this leads to the next cash flow problem: What if you get all the money you need on Day 1?

2. Is Your Small Business Funding Too Much?

Unfortunately, more times than not, having too much money invested in a new product, service, or business can be as detrimental as not having enough money. Sometimes small businesses don't budget properly, and we don't stick to that budget.

Let's say we decide to build a new website. Why not, right? We have the money. Or we find an extremely capable software developer. Yes, some of their skills overlap with existing team members, but they are fantastic, so we hire them. Those fantastic people usually come with a high cost – and you had the skills needed in-house. When you're ready to start advertising, you might ask yourself, why not spend additional money on it? No one will buy our product if they don't know about us. So, you advertise like crazy—even if it blows the budget. Every expense should be looked at through the lens of, "Can this help us move forward? And does the cost outweigh the benefit?"

3. Will Your Cash Flow Support Your Business?

Determining your cash flow starts with your projections. How do you think your business will do? How quickly will customers buy your product/service? Will they come back and buy more? It's important to do a thorough and honest income projection for your business in order to know how much you really have to spend.

The first step in this process is asking...

4. Are Your Sales Estimates Right?

First, you need to break down who your customers are. How long will it take them to find you or try your product? How often will they purchase? Are there seasonal variations to their purchases, like buying more in the summer than the winter? Are there cyclical variations or some other timing involved in the purchase? For example, are they buying a subscription service that renews on a regular basis? Are you selling locally, regionally, or worldwide? Will everyone want your product, or is it based on some other demographic, like male vs. female or older vs. younger?

As you work through these questions, and any others you think of that might be relevant for your particular product/service, you will get a breakdown of your sales profile. Once you have a profile of your customer, you can determine the size of the market you will be entering. Then you can determine the overall percentage of that market you hope to capture. How long will it take to get there? What will be the increase in sales? Be realistic.

Once you have the size of the overall market and a roadmap for sales progression, you should be able to determine customer demand by month and by year going forward. Traditionally, you would put together three- to five-year projections. If you are creating something with a longer ramp-up, you would want to have longer projections. Obviously, the longer the time frame you use, your ability to accurately predict results will diminish, sometimes significantly. That's why the initial projection is just the beginning. As your business is progressing, you will compare actual results to your projected or budgeted figures to determine what variances have occurred and how to adjust your projections with this new information. If there was a one-time event that caused your projections to be off by a lot (for example, a fad cultural event that made one of your products popular for a short period of time), it doesn't make sense to adjust for it happening again. More on this later.

Now you should have sales estimates going out three years, but we need to adjust for variables. So, how confident are you in those estimates? Sixty percent sure? What about the other 40 percent? Is there a 20 percent probability that you will generate that customer revenue much later in the year? Is there a 10 percent chance that sales don't ramp-up this year at all? Is there a 10 percent chance that sales explode? If your answer is yes, then you should adjust your projections based on a change in demand for your product. This sensitivity analysis will allow you to average all of the different probabilities to your base case scenario and come up with a "best guess" for what your sales will look like.

It isn't as difficult as it sounds. In this example, imagine you believe that you will sell 1,000 units in June.

	Base Case	Later in the year	Not at all this year	Sales explode
Probability	60%	20%	10%	10%
Units sold	1000	500	0	1700
(.6x1000) + (.2x500) + (.1x0) + (.1x1700) = 870 units			

When we average these together, we get the best guess of 870 units this year. A little bit more conservative than our 1,000-unit base case estimate, but more realistic, given the uncertainty of our small business.

This gets us back to whether your cash flow will support your business. You have your revenue picture from your sales and customer estimates. You now have to look at your expenses. You first need to put your expenses into two lists—must-haves and like-to-haves. The must-haves are things you cannot do without (think rent, renovations, utilities, employees, office supplies, etc.). Get as detailed as you can. The more detail you have, the easier it will be to uncover spending issues later on. Like-to-haves might also include rent if you start out by working from home but would prefer to have an office. A certain employee might be a like-to-have because they are very talented, but also expensive. Once you've determined your must-haves list, estimate what the cost is for each item. You should concentrate on what actually drives the cost. Is it sales, number of customers, number of employees, number of locations, something else? This will allow you to estimate the cost per $1 or the cost per one unit sold of a product. It will also assist you in estimating the projected cost increases along with sales.

Don't forget taxes—once you are making money, that is. You know the government won't forget either. If you are setting up your business with property or machinery, depreciation will come into account, and so on. Depending on the complexity of your business and your comfort level with accounting, you may want to consider hiring a person to help keep your books and do your taxes.

You've put together your expenses and the drivers that increase or decrease them. This gives you your variable revenues and expenses along with your fixed costs (or overhead such as rent, equipment, vehicles, etc.). You should list them accordingly on your spreadsheet, then take a second step on your income statement by subtracting them from your revenues.

You should now be looking at your net income projections on a monthly and yearly basis. How do they look? If you are like most small businesses, you will need to realize that you will lose money on new products or a new business model for a period of time before sales start to accelerate, and then, hopefully, you will be making money. If your projections show you losing money, even after sales are accelerating, see if you made a mistake with data entry. If you didn't, then you need to take a step back and figure out why. Are costs just too high? If that's the case, can you decrease the costs somehow, or is the venture just not viable? This is an extremely important question to ask. Don't let ego get in your way. If you determine that your business idea isn't actually going to make any money, stopping it before you lost money could be the best decision you ever made. A venture is only right if the numbers say it's right. Your personal biases should not cloud your judgment.

Assuming the numbers support your business idea, what does it look like? When does it show you making money while paying yourself a reasonable salary? If this is six months in, make sure you have enough cash on hand for nine months to a year just to be safe. If it is two years, make sure you have enough cash on hand for three years. The farther in the future your break-even point is, the higher the probability of running short of cash. You want to make sure you don't run into a cash crunch just because things were pushed back by six months or so. As mentioned before, you must remember to pay yourself. You will need to survive, so make sure you personally have enough resources on hand to get through this time period, and not by eating rice cakes and ramen.

5. Are Accounts Receivable and Accounts Payable Causing Your Cash Crunch?

You have your income statement (aka profit and loss statement or P&L). You have a good idea about when you will break even. Are there other things to be looking out for? If you have an existing business and experience a bit of a cash crunch at various times, you should check your accounts receivable. A cash crunch occurs when you unexpectedly become short of cash, and accounts receivable are the amounts customers owe to you. They've already bought your goods or service, but haven't yet paid you, which happens from time to time. Let's say most customers pay their bills within 30 days. Based on that, you start to plan that customers pay within 30 days and you also plan to have enough cash on hand to account for that. What if a customer pays late or starts stretching their payments to 60 days? How about 90 days? Do you have enough cash on hand for that to occur?

Calculating the average number of days that customers take to pay their bills (accounts receivable turnover) can help you get a historical perspective and allow you to project whether customers are stretching to pay you.

Next, look at your accounts receivable on a monthly, semi-annual, and yearly basis, to determine if there is any seasonality to how your customers are paying. You may not view your company as being seasonal, but if your customers or their customers are more seasonal, they may pay you more quickly when cash flow is good, but stretch it out a bit when their cash flow is tighter. It is something to be aware of in running your business.

On your profit and loss statement, you may see what appears to be a negative cash flow even though you know that you're making sales. It makes sense. You sold your product or service, experienced expenses, and received the equivalent of an IOU. There's a gap between the "sale" and the receipt of payment. It's important to remember to bill immediately after delivering your product/service and aggressively pursue payments to keep accounts receivables in check.

Related to that is accounts payable. Accounts payable is what you owe to other people and haven't paid yet. You have permission to pay within 30 days, but, for right now, it shows up on your balance sheet as owing money to someone. This also makes sense because this is another gap. Other companies are letting you buy their product/service, and they are also letting you wait to pay. They are basically loaning you money for that time period. If you stretch out paying them, thus making your accounts payable balance increase, you are effectively taking out a bigger loan for a period of time. From a cash flow perspective, this acts as a positive cash flow, because you are buying more goods or services and not paying for them … yet. In this process, you don't want to stretch payments out too far, as you want to maintain favorable terms with your vendors. (example: Vendor gives a 5 percent discount if you pay within 10 days.) If you consistently pay late, suppliers and vendors will often institute COD or cash-on-demand payment terms in order to continue to do business with them. Accounts payable does give you a little flexibility, though, in dealing with your cash flow.

By taking both accounts receivable and accounts payable into consideration, you have an interrelationship that affects your cash flow. If either one is moving in the wrong direction at any time, your cash flow could be affected. You need to plan for the monthly fluctuations by having a cash cushion and by knowing how much is cash is actually needed. That's why looking at specific categories and customers are so important.

In Summary

We've looked at a number of elements regarding your business's initial funding and cash flow. The documents you'll create in these exercises are not static documents; they are living, changing things. They need to be revisited and adjusted regularly, compared to actual results and updated based on changes that are occurring in your business and industry. Your company's cash flow should be looked at frequently (ideally daily) and compared to projections and budgets at least monthly. This will allow you to stay on top of anything positively or negatively affecting your company's operations. If you stay on top of it and update these documents regularly and routinely, it shouldn't take too much time out of your day. Meanwhile, it will ensure your company stays on firm footing, so you can minimize the probability of any cash crunches and keep cash flowing.

Payment Priorities Revisited:

When small businesses become desperate for cash, and there are no other funding sources besides personal savings, the stress levels in your family can become stratospheric.

I was in a cash crunch with my first small business, Sales Sherpas, during the second year of operation. I had paid our taxes, had to move an employee from full-time pay to part-time pay, negotiated an extra 60 days to pay our office rent, and negotiated some advance payments on new client projects. However, even after taking those actions, I was unable to pay myself and bring home income for my family for six months. I went months without a good night's sleep. It created a great deal of stress on my relationship with my wife and strain on my family—not just financially, but psychologically as well.

Fortunately, my wife and I had put a plan in place where we could live on her income, although things would be very tight. We stopped making payments into our kids' college funds, stopped taking our annual vacations, minimized meals out, and when we did go out with friends (who had traditional jobs), I would suggest less expensive restaurants or just order a pizza or takeout. Eventually, the company started generating cash and the financial cloud was lifted for me personally, but I promised myself to be more careful with company cash in the future.

I discussed payment priorities briefly before, but this is critically important to your family and small business, so we are going to revisit payment priorities with a little more detail.

Payment Priorities for Small Businesses:

Priority #1: The Government (taxes, licenses, and other fees) - The government does not take kindly to not receiving their revenue and can shut down your business. If you don't pay them, your goose is cooked. Game over.

Priority #2: Your Employees - Effective organizations live and die based on people. Pay your people. If times get tight, move them to part-time, or perhaps move them into contractor roles.

Priority #3: Your Suppliers - You might have critical suppliers of materials. Perhaps you have to have an office space. I find that many small businesses overspend for office space. Starting at your home is one way to go, but there is a great deal to be said for the camaraderie of a small business incubator or other shared workspaces. Be creative but make sure that your vendors and suppliers are paid, and paid on time.

Priority #4: Yourself - That's right. Your paycheck will be driven by how well you and your small business are performing. But, if you don't pay all of the aforementioned parties, you won't stay in business.

Following those payment priorities might seem intuitive now. But actually, living by them is an entirely different proposition. When cash flow is tight, be prepared, because at some point you will be faced with a difficult decision about who won't be getting paid or who will have to wait to get paid. At some point, that party will be you.

The pain of being paid last will quickly fade when your business thrives and you reap the benefits. Only small businesses understand the sacrifices that are made to create a living, breathing, and a thriving company. Hang on to that quiet confidence and just smile.

Restart Insight: When you are the small business owner, you get paid last.

Step 10 – Pivoting to Thrive

As you can imagine successful business models do not remain the same over time. Successful small businesses need to adapt to new environments in order to thrive.

Pivot – A fundamental change to a business model such as pursuing new customer segments, building new channels of distribution, adding new revenue models, etc.

Knowing when to pivot is very important. Your Business Model Canvas helps guide these decisions because, if you need to make changes to or adjust any element of the business model, all the information is there, at your fingertips.

Interview: Kevin Kauffman, Small Business Development Center

Kevin Kauffman, from the Small Business Development Center (SBDC) at the University of Wisconsin-Whitewater, has seen scores of small businesses come through his office for help. In the U.S., the SBDC is a network of over 1,300 consultants in 62 different networks. It is the largest small business consulting network in the nation. Kevin has personally consulted to thousands of small businesses on how to maximize growth and their bottom-line. I asked him about the common links he sees amongst small businesses that thrive long-term.

"The common links I see amongst these thriving small businesses that really last are that they are always looking for new opportunities, they react quickly to those opportunities and their competitors simply can't keep up. They are always ready to pivot their business model. They say, "where do we want to be and how can we get there?". They are not reactive - they are the epitome of being proactive. These innovative small businesses are always looking for new ways to gain market share, pick-up new geographies, buy other companies, and build out new products and services. I am seeing these innovative small businesses are piloting new products

and services now, during this crisis. So, when more customers come back they will really take-off. They did the same thing during the economic collapse of 2008. This mentality is baked into the way they think, their culture. They can survive virtually anything."

Here are some examples of how a small business could successively pivot to help their business thrive.

Example 1: Competitors Lower Their Prices

Situation: Your main competitor just dropped their prices by 10%. Your customers are calling you to see if you are lowering your prices as well.

Your Options:

1. **Lower price with no change**: Lower your price to match your competition but keep costs the same. This is easy but could be very dangerous if it results in a price war. In the meantime, you are lowering your profit margins.

2. **Lower price and cut costs:** Lower your price but cut costs, and perhaps quality or customer service, to maintain your profit margin. You have not created a hit to your bottom-line but have simply been reactive and the drop-in customer service and quality will, eventually, negatively impact your sales.

3. **Focus on quality and customer service:** Communicate to your customers proactively through your branding and marketing that you are a premium brand. You have the best customer service and the best quality. If customers want to leave then, as painful as it might be, you need to let them go. If this trend threatens your business model it is probably time to reevaluate your customer segments or product/service offerings. You need to pivot.

Example 2: Lower Retail Traffic

Situation: Customers who used to come into your retail store on a regular basis are now simply purchasing substitute products on Amazon.

Your Options:

1. **Hold a sale:** Lower your prices and promote a sale. This can create more traffic in the short-run but having discounts in the long-run desensitizes customers to future discounts and lowers the perception of brand quality and customer service.

2. **Reduce your product selection:** You might indeed be offering products that have a low-profit margin and you are simply tying up cash unnecessarily in inventory that isn't moving. This could help but also might further diminish customer's desire to come to your store and buy other more profitable products as well

3. **Build or rebuild your Ecommerce site**: If you have a retail store and you don't have an Ecommerce store your small business is probably going to go the way of the buggy whip. If you don't have an Ecommerce store simply use a user-friendly service such as Shopify to quickly create a fully functional way for your customers to purchase your products directly through you

Example 3: Safe Distancing Reducing Restaurant Capacity

Situation: The safe distancing requirements, customer desires, and perhaps your concerns are leading to a significant reduction in your restaurant capacity even after you open up again.

Your Options:

1. **Ride it out:** Just rely on slow increases in traffic within the restaurant.
2. **Add outdoor dining:** Create a low-cost outdoor patio or other space to off-set the lower capacity within the restaurant.
3. **At-home delivery:** Quickly test a service such as EatStreet to deliver food right to your customer's door. You get incremental revenue but have none of the labor costs, transportation costs, or liability of your own delivery service. Keep in mind that these services or individuals become represent your company, so select a service carefully.

Interview: Craig Jorgensen, VJS Construction Services

Regarding pivoting, I spoke with Craig Jorgensen, the President of VJS Construction Services. VJS specializes in developing facilities for education, senior living, housing, retail, manufacturing, medical, corporate office, religion, and government. They also have new divisions that provide real estate services and renewable energy construction services. Craig discussed how his firm got through the economic collapse of 2008 and how that experience changed his perspective on how to handle crises, including, most recently, the Coronavirus pandemic.

"Our firm has seen a great deal and survived through many crises. The original company began in 1918 and weathered the great depression, closed down in 1974. My father bought into what is now VJS in 1976. We also got through the 2008 meltdown.

Based on our insights from previous crises in real estate we saw the 2008 meltdown before it occurred. So, we acted in advance. Our first move was to jump into survival mode and cut overhead. But then we realized we needed to take a look at the marketplace and how to capitalize on the market and opportunities it presented. One of the new markets we got into was the construction of airplane hangars for corporate jets. Corporations had to manage concerns that executives had about their personal safety and they also looked at the value of a CEO's time. If that CEO can leave in the morning and be back in the afternoon they can save sometimes an entire day of travel. That provides a tremendous productivity increase for corporations.

I also learned from 2008 to look two years ahead and try to anticipate the market and look for these opportunities. Based on COVID and the specific impact of people working at home, the demand for office space is going to shrink. So, we are focusing efforts on the service side of our business and renewables. We are staffing-up and focusing our marketing and sales efforts in those areas and reducing those costs in the areas of traditional new construction. The last and probably the most important strategy we use is focusing energy on our employees and families first. If you take care of employees and their families they will in turn take care of your customers which helps your company."

In Conclusion

I truly hope that *Restart* has provided you with the tools and inspiration to think differently during times of chaos. You have acquired insights and knowledge that you can directly apply to make your small business thrive.

Creating a thriving business is not easy. You need to be willing to take an objective look at your current business model, talk with your current and prospective customers, explore new business models, develop new products and services, consider new branding and marketing, protect your company with legal resources, recruit and retain the best team, implement effective and efficient software, incorporate Ecommerce and pivot your business model as necessary.

Most of your competitors will either "dive" or "survive." They will sell their businesses, close down or simply slash their overhead. This will be the lowest risk in the short-run but will most likely be lethal to their businesses in the long-run. You now know better. **Now you know how to "thrive."** It is now time for you to implement this knowledge and turn it into skills that you and your team can use to create a sustainable competitive advantage.

...and now it is time for you and your small business to THRIVE!

— G

PS: If you want to help your team members acquire this knowledge get them a copy of *Restart*. You can reinforce this knowledge with our new, powerful, practical, free videos, training, and books at **restartsmallbiz.com**, and on Facebook, Twitter and Instagram.

Glossary

This section contains terminology that every modern small business owner needs to understand. It is also a way to impress your family, friends, other business leaders, academics, and your team members!

Accelerator (or Small Business Accelerator) - Formal program whereby small businesses spend time with mentors who provide coaching, networking, financial investment, and typically incubator space in return for a portion of equity in the Small Business. Accelerators typically receive 5-10 percent equity for their services upfront, sometimes with the option to purchase additional equity in the future. Accelerators are not be confused with incubators which are physical spaces, not programs.

AWS (Amazon Web Services) - Subsidiary of Amazon that provides on-demand cloud computing platforms and APIs to individuals, companies, and governments, on a metered pay-as-you-go basis.

Android - Android is a mobile operating system based on a modified version of the Linux and other open-source software, designed primarily for touchscreen mobile devices such as smartphones and tablets. Android is primarily used on non-iOS (Apple) devices such as Google, LG, Motorola, Samsung smartphones, laptops, and tablet computers.

Angel Investor (aka Angel) - Individual or group of individuals that invest money into startups, typically in exchange for equity. The most high-profile example of an angel investor is "The Sharks" on ABC's Shark Tank.

Acqui-hire - Acquisition of a company for the purposes of hiring their employees—not for the intrinsic value of the company.

Balance Sheet - Summary of the financial balances of an individual or organization, whether it be a sole proprietorship, a business partnership, a corporation, a private limited company, or other organization such as Government or not-for-profit entities. Assets, liabilities, and ownership equity are listed as of a specific date, such as the end of its financial year. A standard company balance sheet has two sides: assets on the left, and financing on the right–which itself has two parts; liabilities and ownership equity.

Big Box Retailers - Physically large retail establishment, usually part of a chain of stores.

Bootstrapping – The act of self-funding a startup. This can be funding that comes from the founder(s). Sometimes raising, friends/fools/family is considered bootstrapping.

Brick and Mortar Businesses - Physical presence of an organization or business in a building or other structure. The term *brick-and-mortar business* is often used to refer to a company that possesses or leases retail shops, factory production facilities, or warehouses for its operations.

Burn Rate (or "burn") - Rate at which a startup or small business spends money. Typically measured per month. For example: If a company has a burn of $100,000 that would typically represent using $100,000 a month in cash. When burn rates increase at an unsustainable rate, investors can get nervous. The investors are left with a situation where they need the company to increase profits or investors need to put in more money to sustain the burn.

Business Model - All of the methods used by a company to deliver value to its customers.

Business Plan - Document that describes the business model in detail. Some investors will say that "business plans are dead or a waste of time; just create a pitch deck." However, this oversimplifies the value gained by asking difficult questions about how the startup or small business will be organized, grown, and managed.

CARES Act - The CARES Act signed into law on March 27, 2020, gives states the option of extending unemployment compensation to independent contractors and other workers who are ordinarily ineligible for unemployment benefits.

Cash Flow Statement - A financial statement that summarizes the amount of cash and cash equivalents entering and leaving a company. The cash flow statement measures how well a company manages its cash position, meaning how well the company generates cash to pay its debt obligations and fund its operating expenses.

C Corp - Corporate structure where its profits are taxed separately from its owners under sub-step C of the Internal Revenue Code.

Company - Self-sustaining organization composed of synergistic people and resources.

Convertible Note - Short-term loan made by investors that converts into equity based on an established milestone (e.g. valuation of the startup in a later funding round).

Copyright - Legal right of ownership of original work, used to protect literary works, live performances, photographs, movies, and software (although rarely used for software).

Cost of Acquisition (CAC) - Generally calculated as the total cost that reflects the marketing and sales costs divided by the number of new customers over a defined period of time. At the beginning of the small business lifecycle, these costs are typically very high due to significant sales and marketing costs relative to new customers acquired.

Crowdfunding - Crowdfunding is the process of raising capital to fund a small business, product, invention, project, literary work, event, or special cause. This is usually done through a web-based campaign on a specific crowdfunding platform. There are four types of crowdfunding platforms: Reward Crowdfunding, Equity Crowdfunding, Donation Crowdfunding, and Debt Crowdfunding. Examples of Crowdfunding services include Kickstarter, Indiegogo, and Kiva.

Customer -An individual or group that PAYS you money for your product or services. Don't confuse a customer with a USER of your product or service. The marketing messages can be very different from customers and users. For example: If a parent pays for their daughter's cellular service but she uses the cellular service (through her smartphone). The customer's primary need to provide safety for the daughter while the daughter's desire is probably just to communicate with friends, family, and work.

Ecommerce - Commercial transactions conducted electronically on the Internet. This could be businesses that have their Ecommerce website or through a service such as Amazon or Etsy.

Early State Company - A small business that has matured to the point when market validation has been achieved, but process improvement and team expansion are required for the company to scale.

Economic Injury Disaster Loan (EIDL) - In response to the Coronavirus (COVID-19) pandemic, small businesses in all U.S. states, Washington D.C., and territories were able to apply for an Economic Injury Disaster Loan advance of up to $10,000. This advance is designed to provide economic relief to businesses that are currently experiencing a temporary loss of revenue. This loan advance will not have to be repaid. These loans may be used to pay fixed debts, payroll, accounts payable and other bills that can't be paid because of the disaster's impact. The interest rate is 3.75% for small businesses. The interest rate for non-profits is 2.75%. You can only apply for EIDL loans through SBA.gov (you cannot apply through SBA.com)

Equity - The amount of ownership, typically represented as a percentage, that an individual or organization owns in business.

Exit – Sale of an organization for, ideally, a significant amount of cash or equity in another company. This is why individuals such as angels and Venture Capitalists (VCs) give you money. They need a return on their investment, just like you do on your investments. The other form of exit is shutting down the company.

FBA (Fulfilled by Amazon) - Fulfillment By Amazon (FBA) is a service provided by Amazon that provides storage, packing, and shipping assistance to sellers.

Fixed Costs – Costs that are constant whatever the number of goods or services produced. Examples include rent, company vehicles, office equipment.

Fixed Mindset - In a fixed mindset, people believe their qualities are fixed traits and therefore cannot change.

Future-Proofing - Future-proofing is the process of anticipating the future and developing methods of minimizing the effects of shocks and stresses of future events.

Gig Economy - An economy where growth is driven by the use of independent contractors vs. traditional employees. Example: Uber's drivers are classified as contractors and help contribute to the "gig economy."

Google Docs - Google Docs is a word processor included as part of a free, web-based software office suite offered by Google within its Google Drive service.

Google Drive - A file storage and synchronization service developed by Google.

Google Sheets - Google Sheets is a spreadsheet program included as part of a free, web-based software office suite offered by Google within its Google Drive service.

Google Slides - Presentation program included as part of a free, web-based software office suite offered by Google within its Google Drive service.

Growth Mindset - Mindset that is based on the belief that your basic qualities are things you can cultivate through your efforts.

Income Statement – Or profit and loss statement(P&L), is one of the financial statements of a company and shows the company's revenues and expenses during a particular period. It indicates how the revenues are transformed into the net income or net profit.

Incubator - Physical space where small businesses congregate, collaborate, and manage their startups. Sometimes people confuse accelerators with incubators. Accelerators are programs, incubators are places. Frequently, accelerators can be located in incubators. For example, TechStars in Chicago is located in the 1871 incubator and Launch Pad is based in the Whitewater Incubation Center.

Intellectual Property (IP) - Refers to ideas, including inventions, music, and literature. IP falls into three categories:

> • **Patents** are a form of intellectual property that gives its owner the legal right to exclude others from making, using, selling, and importing an invention for a limited period of years, in exchange for publishing an enabling public disclosure of the invention.
>
> **There are two types of patents:**
>
> > • **Utility patents** are patents that provide legal protection to the creation of a new or improved—and useful—product, process, or machine.

- **Design patents** are patents that provide legal protection granted to the ornamental design of a functional item. Design patents are a type of industrial design right.

- **Copyrights** are legal rights of ownership to original work, used to protect literary works, live performances, photographs, movies, and software (although rarely used for software).

- **Trademarks** are a type of intellectual property consisting of a recognizable sign, design, or expression which identifies products or services of a particular source.

iOS – A mobile operating system created and developed by Apple Inc. exclusively for its hardware. It is the operating system that presently powers many of the company's mobile devices, including the iPhone.

Friends and Family- Two traditional external sources of investment capital available to many entrepreneurs and small businesses.

Linux - Linux is a family of open-source Unix-like operating systems based on the Linux kernel, an operating system kernel first released on September 17, 1991

Limited Liability Company (LLC) - Corporate structure whereby the members of the company cannot be held personally liable for the company's debts or responsibilities. Limited liability companies are considered a hybrid between corporations and sole proprietorships.

Minimum Viable Product (MVP) - Most basic feature set in a product or service to determine if your value proposition resonates with prospective customers. The big trap first-time small businesses fall into is adding features and functionality that are not required and convoluting the insights that need to be acquired.

Monthly Recurring Revenue (MRR) - Represents the measure of monthly revenue for service providers and typically Software-as-a-Service (SaaS) providers.

Non-Compete Agreement (Non-Compete) - Agreement between two parties (e.g. employee and employer) whereby one party (e.g. employee) agrees not to work for or create an entity that competes with the other party (e.g. the previous employer).

Non-Disclosure Agreement (NDA) - Agreement between two parties whereby "the disclosing party" provides proprietary information to "the receiving party" and restricts the sharing of the proprietary information with third parties. Don't ask angel investors to sign NDAs—they won't, and you will lose credibility.

Omnichannel - retailing concept of selling your products through the sales channels and technologies where and when your customers want to buy.

Operating Agreement - An agreement between the members of a Limited Liability Company (LLC) that governs the business, including member powers, rights, duties, and obligations. It also outlines the decision-making process related to operational, functional, and financial issues in a structured manner. The operating agreement of LLC companies is similar to bylaws used by corporations.

Overhead - Expenses are all costs on the income statement except for direct labor, direct materials, and direct expenses. **Overhead** expenses include accounting fees, advertising, insurance, interest, legal fees, labor burden, rent, repairs, supplies, taxes, telephone bills, travel expenditures, and utilities.

Pitch - Brief presentation, typically under twenty minutes, whereby small businesses present a rapid overview of their business model to prospective investors or other interested parties.

Pitch Deck - Series of electronic slides, usually under twenty, that displays the elements of a business model.

Pivot – Fundamental change to a business model such as pursuing new customer segments, building new channels of distribution, adding new revenue models, etc.

Pro Formas - Forward-looking financial documents, such as pro forma cash flow statements and pro forma income statements (profit and loss statements) based on hypothetical conditions.

Profit and Loss Statement(P&L) – See Income Statement definition.

Runway - How long, usually measured in months, a startup has before it runs out of cash.

SBA (Small Business Administration) - The U.S. Small Business Administration is a United States government agency that provides support to small businesses and small businesses.

SBDC (Small Business Development Center) – A nationwide network of Small Business Development Centers. It is the most comprehensive small business assistance network in the United States and its territories. SBDCs are hosted by leading universities, colleges, state economic development agencies, and private partners. It is partially funded through the SBA.

Software as a Service (SaaS) - Software that is provided as an ongoing service, as opposed to a traditional initial outlay to purchase a software package. This pricing model is particularly appealing to small- and medium-sized businesses (SMBs) that don't traditionally have the budget to make large software purchases. SaaS companies have particular appeal to angel investors and venture capital firms based on the consistent and compounding effect of revenue.

S Corp - Corporate structure where profits are passed on to the shareholders and taxed on their personal returns.

Scale - Achieving rapid customer adoption (growth) while simultaneously expanding the organization and refining processes to maintain growth.

Seed Capital - The initial investments made in a startup by someone other than the founder(s).

Series A (or A Round) - A small business's first significant round of funding, which is typically funded by angels.

Series B, C, D, etc. - The subsequent rounds of investments in a Small Business.

Software Engineer - Individual who designs, develops, tests, and maintains the software. Unless you want software engineers to increase their fees and hold you in complete contempt for ignorance, don't call them programmers.

Small Business - Business size standard, which is usually stated in the number of employees or average annual receipts, represents the largest size that a business (including its subsidiaries and affiliates) may be to remain classified as a small business for SBA and federal contracting programs. The definition of "small" varies by industry. A common definition is a company employing 500 people or less.

Startup Idea - Series of hypotheses created with the goal of formulating a small business.

Term Sheet - Non-binding agreement between a small business owner and investor that ultimately is incorporated into investment agreements (such as an operating agreement).

Trademark - Can be a word, phrase, symbol, and/or design that identifies and distinguishes the source of the goods (products) of one party from those of others. Typically, we think of brands, logos, icons, and taglines in the small business world when discussing trademarks.

User - Person or organization that consumes a product or service provided by an organization (small business, early-stage, or mature organization). Users are not to be confused with customers. Customers pay for goods and services but they may not be the users of your goods and services.

User Interface (UI) - Series of screens, pages, buttons, and images displayed on a screen (such as a smartphone, laptop, or monitor).

User Experience (UX) - The process that a user goes through when interacting with a service (e.g. software) or a product.

Value Proposition - Statement a business or other organization uses to describe the way it will help its customers.

Variable Costs - Costs that vary with the level of output. For example, the cost of ingredients in a meal being sold by a restaurant.

Venture Capital - Investment made by a group of accredited investors provided by funds or specific firms, typically in exchange for equity.

Venture Capitalists - Individuals who invest in early-stage companies (post-startup phase). Angel investors invest in startups (pre-early-stage companies).

Wantrepreneur - Individual that has a business idea, but never executes to turn the idea into a proven business model.

About the Author

Restart is Dave's third book and was written to help small businesses thrive during times of chaos and build new skills to adapt and thrive during any future upheavals to their business models. *The College Student Small Business Guide* was his second book and written to help college students to launch successful startups while still in college and was an Amazon Best Seller. The first book Gee wrote was *The Corporate Refugee Small Business Guide* to help mid-career professionals launch their startups while balancing their family.

Dave taught in the MBA program at the University of Wisconsin-Madison. He currently teaches and is a Director Launch Pad startup accelerator at the University of Wisconsin-Whitewater. He mentors startups at gener8tor, a national leading accelerator. Dave also mentors small businesses to help them maximize their profitable growth. Dave spent over 20 years working in sales and marketing roles for Fortune 500 companies including Motorola, BellSouth, U.S. Cellular, TDS, and Humana.

After leaving the corporate world, he launched his first small business, Sales Sherpas, an advertising agency. Dave then co-founded and was the CEO of Bungee, which provided a software-as-a-service loyalty program. Next, he co-founded Classmunity, a web-based fundraising management system for school districts.

He is currently researching new initiatives and technologies to help improve mental health of teenagers and young adults.

Dave founded Startup Guides which provides consulting and publishing services for startups and small businesses. Startup Guides is the parent company of Restart Small Biz. Restart Small Biz is a new service that provides small business growth strategies with free resources, articles, videos and training.

He earned his MBA from Marquette University and his BBA from the University of Wisconsin-Whitewater.

Dave lives with his family near Lake Geneva, Wisconsin. He enjoys mountain biking, boating, cruising in his convertible, and hiking with his family and loyal lab, Caesar.

Continue to Make Your Small Business Thrive!

Connect with to receive free articles, posts, videos and training to help your small business thrive.

Website: restartsmallbiz.com
Facebook: restartsmallbiz
Twitter: @restartsmallbiz
Instagram: @restartsmallbiz

Connect directly with Dave!

Email: dave@restartsmallbiz.com
LinkedIn: davidrgee